Rental Property Investing

Learn the Secrets to Invest Smart, Generate Passive Income, and Achieve Your Financial Freedom with Rental Property Investing

Sean Copson

© **Copyright 2019 by Sean Copson- All rights reserved.**

The content contained within this book may not be reproduced, duplicated or transmitted without direct written permission from the author or the publisher.

Under no circumstances will any blame or legal responsibility be held against the publisher, or author, for any damages, reparation, or monetary loss due to the information contained within this book, either directly or indirectly.

Legal Notice:

This book is copyright protected. It is only for personal use. You cannot amend, distribute, sell, use, quote or paraphrase any part, or the content within this book, without the consent of the author or publisher.

Disclaimer Notice:

Please note the information contained within this document is for educational and entertainment purposes only. All effort has been executed to present accurate, up to date, reliable, complete information. No warranties of any kind are declared or implied. Readers acknowledge that the author is not engaging in the rendering of legal, financial, medical or professional advice. The content within this book has been derived from various sources. Please consult a licensed professional before attempting any techniques outlined in this book.

By reading this document, the reader agrees that under no circumstances is the author responsible for any losses, direct or indirect, that are incurred as a result of the use of information contained within this document, including, but not limited to, errors, omissions, or inaccuracies.

Table of Contents

Table of Contents 4

Introduction *1*

    Introspection..............................2

    Time 4

Chapter 1: What Is an Investment Property 6

  Why Do You Want It? 7

    What Does Taking Action Mean? 9

Chapter 2: To Be Successful Is an Inside Job *11*

  Have a Plan 12

    Attitude 13

    Perseverance 14

    Flexibility 15

  Understanding the Basics.................. 16

    Identifying Your Comfort Zone 17

  Treat It Like a Business Not a Hobby. 18

    Imagine 18

    Financial Goals 19

- Vision, Mission, and Values 19
- **Setting SMART Goals** **20**
- **Success** **22**
  - Stay Positive 22
  - Do Your Research 25
- *Chapter 3: Understanding Investment Properties* ***28***
  - **Types of Investment Properties** **29**
    - Single-family Residence 29
    - Multi-family Residence 30
    - Condominiums (Condos) 31
    - Townhomes 32
    - Foreclosures 32
  - **Location, Location, Location** **33**
    - Class A 34
    - Class B 35
    - Class C 35
  - **Other Things to Consider:** **36**
    - Crime/Drugs 36
    - Schools 36
    - Jobs & Unemployment Rate 37
    - Population Growth 38

Transportation 39
Amenities/Trends 39

Chapter 4: Analyzing a Rental Property *41*

Speculating **42**
Return on Investment (ROI) **43**
The Cost Method 44
The Out-Of-Pocket Method 45

What Is Income? **46**
What Is an Expense? **47**
Vacancy Rates 49
Repairs 49
Capital Expenditures 50

What Makes a "Good" Rental Property? **53**
Attributes 54
Problems to Consider 57
Financial Considerations 61

Chapter 5: Tax Implications *65*
United States **65**
Income 66
Expenses 67

Canada **68**
    Expenses 68
    Capital Cost Allowance 71

Chapter 6: Financing Investment Properties *73*
  Leveraging vs. All Cash **73**
    Pros for Leveraging 76
    Cons for Leveraging................................... 76
    Pros for All Cash 77
    Cons for All Cash 78
  Portfolio Lenders **79**
  Private Lenders **80**
  Getting Creative.................................**82**
    Home Equity..82
    Partnerships 83
    House Hacking 84

Chapter 7: Making an Offer *87*
  Through Multiple Listing Service (MLS) Listings...**87**
  Offering on a Property Not Listed on MLS... **88**
  Earnest Money Deposit......................**89**

What Should Your Offer Include? 91

How Much Should You Offer? 92

Chapter 8: Negotiations 96

Negotiation Process 96

When to Negotiate 99

   Tips for Successful Negotiations 100

Chapter 9: Due Diligence 104

Title Search 104

Document Inspection 106

Physical Inspection 110

   Other Inspections You May Want to Consider 112

   After the Inspection 115

Chapter 10: Closing the Sale 116

Insurance 116

   Insurance for Landlords 117

   Setting Up Your Bank Accounts 120

   Forms 121

   Preparing Bookkeeping 123

To LLC or Not to LLC 123

   LLC Benefits 124

   Problems with an LLC 124

Chapter 11: You Own, So What's Next? 126

Self Management vs. Property Management Company 126

- Role of a Property Manager 127
- Pros 127
- Cons 128
- No One Will Care Like You 129
- Self Management 130

Get the Property Ready to Rent 130

Chapter 12: Additional Resources 132

Accounting 132
Property Management 133
Building Inspectors 134
Miscellaneous 135

Conclusion 138

Some Last Things to Consider 139
Final Thoughts 141

Citations 146

Introduction

The year was 1978. In South London, an elderly woman's precious cat ran up a tree and could not get down. She begged and pleaded with the cat for hours but soon discovered it was hopeless. Finally, she called the local fire station to request help. The firemen came to help the poor woman and had cleverly devised a plan to get the cat out of the tree. The ladder went up, and the cat came down in the arms of a heroic fireman. The neighbors cheered, the elderly woman was full of joy, and the firemen rejoiced in their accomplishment. The elderly woman treated the heroes to some afternoon tea, which they graciously accepted. As the afternoon waned, and the firemen took their leave, the woman said a final goodbye. Still celebrating their successful rescue and discussing the afternoon they unexpectedly enjoyed, the firemen backed out of the driveway—only to run over and kill the cat.

Now this may just be an anecdote I found during my research, it is an entirely appropriate way to start the book because something like this can happen without due diligence.

You spend all this time crossing T's and dotting I's only to have some small things derail the process because you got cocky about a deal or sloppy with an inspection. No matter how smart or talented you are, things happen. Whether you missed a huge problem during the walkthrough, hired the wrong property manager or allowed bad tenants to move in. You *must* be diligent with rental property investments.

Introspection

Real estate is an investment, not only in money but in time. Yes, it can provide stability, and regular returns if done correctly. But before all that can take place, you need to engage in some serious introspection. What made you first look at one deal over another? Is this something you need or want? Will this produce the monetary and potentially emotional returns you were hoping? Will this deal require any sacrifices, such as relocation, or a lot of extra time?

While this all may sound a little 'woo' to you, the reality is that you have to know what you want and why you want it. Knowing these things comes with understanding who you are. Do a little soul searching to discover your true beliefs and values. What is that you truly hold dear, to run a business and understand your boundaries and belief system and values take work and a deep knowing of you who you are. If this isn't something you've ever done or considered it won't be easy. But it will separate the successful business owners from the unsuccessful ones.

What I found in my research was that a lot of people with a high net worth hold the belief that you must engage in some form of personal development. This isn't to say that you need to start buying healing crystals online or get your palm read, but it does mean knowing who you are, what you believe, and be willing to learn.

If you aren't willing to learn through reading or finding a mentor, then you may be chasing that elusive dream of being financially free, forever. No man is an island.

This book is meant to help you navigate the world of real estate and understand its not just about finding the best deals but why you are doing it in the first place. These easy terms will get you to that first, second, or third property and start building that empire of your dreams.

If you are reading this and intending for this book to assist you in buying your first piece of investment, then here is your formal welcome into the world of real estate investing. If you are already have some properties under your belt, then I hope to enlighten you with new tips and tricks you can utilize during your next purchase.

Time

Before we get started on investing, one thing I want you to consider is time. This is your most precious commodity, so you need to spend it wisely in the pursuit of real estate investments.

Don't let your current situation, no matter how unsatisfactory, dictate how you spend your time. Don't let it convince you that if you work a little harder, go further into debt, and risk losing money on a deal, that it's worth doing something you end up hating. Know that spending time away from your family for extended periods probably won't make you happier in the long run, especially if one of your reasons for doing this is to benefit them.

Spend some time questioning why you are chasing this deal. Does it feel right? Does it align with the goals, vision, and mission you have for yourself?

Before investing your time chasing a deal that doesn't fit or takes you places that ultimately make you unhappy, even if it brings you success, start to question where you are putting your efforts. Does this give you more time or take it away? If part of the reason for starting this adventure in real estate investing is to gain time with family, that should always be your motivation behind deals.

I hope that as you make your way through this book, you will realize why you want to start investing in real estate. Once you have answers to the important questions, then you have attained some of the basics and practical tools to get there.

Thanks again for choosing this book, make sure you leave a brief review on Amazon if you like it, I'd really like to know what you think.

Chapter 1: What Is an Investment Property

"Opportunities don't happen. You create them."
- Chris Grosse

An investment property is real estate purchased for the sole intent of earning a return on that investment either through rental earnings, the sale of the property, aka flipping, or a combination of both. The property can be held by an individual investor, a group of investors, or a corporation. But, for this book, I am focusing on you, the individual, as a single investor.

Real estate can provide stable, secure returns on an ongoing basis through monthly rent or yearly leases, which is why a lot of people in these uncertain times are turning to real estate to secure financial freedom or retirement padding. Such as short term investing or "flipping" that require minimal work and maximum profit.

The last option is buying large or small chunks of undeveloped land and keeping it for development. This would mean you leasing it as necessary and build up more capital that way. For this scenario, you do need deep pockets as there can be unexpected and expensive setbacks, even with something undeveloped. However, the payoff of going this route can be substantial.

Why Do You Want It?

Deciding to start investing in real estate is an admirable goal. Set goals for yourself while getting started. Without a plan, the target can disappear, and having a 'why' for this goal brings it to life and provides the motivation to continue when things may not be happening as quickly as you would like.

Goals and dreams can quickly go by the wayside when things get tough, or you are knocked off your axis by some bump in the road. Having a reason is stronger and keeps you focused on the result. Also, consider the feelings behind these goals. How do you ultimately want to feel when these goals start to become a reality? Attaching emotion to them makes it more real in your mind. If you tell yourself enough times that something is yours then in most cases, you will convince your brain and start to believe.

Is your 'why' so that you can leave your 9-5 job? To make more money and gain financial freedom? Are you looking to invest more in your retirement? Maybe it's to be able to spend more time with your kids or grandkids. Is it as simple as wanting to succeed at something new? If so, you need to define what it means for you to achieve, figure out benchmarks to signal you're on the right track.

Knowing your reason will keep you focused on the result, keeping your eye on the prize. There will be times when you will have to weigh the deal against how it impacts your outcome. If the agreement negatively affects any of the reasons why you started investing in the first place, if it will make your life or those in it miserable, then walk away! It's not the right arrangement for you.

Whatever your reasons are, you need to declare them. Make a list of 'why' and 'why not' and say them loud, proud, and often. Some go through life wishing, and others make it happen. Which one are you? Daydreaming is a great way to pass the time, but depending on why you want to start investing in real estate, you should already be making it happen. As Napoleon Hill wrote in his book *Think and Grow Rich,* "What the mind can conceive and believe, it can achieve."

What Does Taking Action Mean?

It means getting up and changing your world. It means doing it for yourself because no one else is going to do it for you. Be willing to spend all of your free time thinking about investing, doing research, and finding your specific way to make it happen. There is no one right way to go about investing. Through your research find a way that makes sense for you and your goals. Then start laying out some action steps that you can implement to get started.

Replace your daydreams of extra money with real strategies and be willing to invest what you do have to produce gains. It means understanding that this is not a get-rich-quick type of endeavor. It takes time, dedication, and perseverance. Investing is consistent action over long periods, staying committed and doing what needs to be done. Even when it feels like you haven't made any progress, it's the accumulation of small actions that will get to your end goal.

Lastly, it means being prepared for the not so glamorous side of investing and owning properties, such as having to deal with difficult people, piles of paperwork, no breaks, and the looming possibility of losing your investment.

Before I ultimately turn you off of investing in real estate, let me say this, investing in anything brings with it some risk, you can't get away from that. Yes, a lot of people may not be successful at running a business through their rental property, but there are ways of decreasing that risk.

Chapter 2: To Be Successful Is an Inside Job

"Would you like me to give you the formula for success? It's quite simple, really. Double your rate of failure. You are thinking of failure as the enemy of success. But it isn't at all. You can be discouraged by failure, or you can learn from it, so go ahead and make mistakes. Make all you can. Because remember that's where you will find success."

- Thomas J Watson

Success for most of us boils down to money. Neither good nor bad; money merely reflects our values. Money provides us with choices, and the more we have, the more things we can consider and open more doors. It might be getting 'woo' for you again, but honestly, the more defined your values are, and the stronger your belief system is, you will start to realize your choices determine your life. And positive choices make you more likely to pursue positive experiences. This is enlightenment to wealth and how a lot of the wealthy view life.

Think of it this way: The more money you have, the more good you can do. Maybe you buy a complex that saves a person in need from foreclosure, or support low-income housing to keep families off the street.

Where you put your energy, the money will flow. Understanding that money is good because of all the good it can do will help you on your journey to financial freedom. Financial freedom is about personal growth—you need to grow with your finances, or they won't last. Be aware of the new skills and greater wisdom you need to continue moving forward.

Have a Plan

Taking into consideration what you want to accomplish with this financial freedom, you now need a plan. Keep in mind, my intention is not going to look like yours, but everyone who takes on any big goal will need a strategy to begin moving forward, or you may as well push it aside as a pipe dream.

The three most significant pieces to the investment planning puzzle are attitude, perseverance, and flexibility. These three elements will carry you through when you are discouraged over how much longer it takes to find and buy a place than you initially thought or if your plan isn't working out the way you envisioned.

Attitude

Finding that first property can be stressful. The time it takes for the right one to come along can take time. It might even get discouraging. Developing a "can do" attitude that you will find the right one will come in handy in more ways than one. It's better to do your homework and wait for the smart investment property to surface than risk buying the wrong one that ruins you financially. You will be less likely to make an impulsive decision that can put you in a sticky situation and cause unnecessary trouble.

This can be said whether it's your first property or your thirtieth, attitude will get you far. Never take it for granted that the right property is just around the corner because the market can be volatile. Always maintain an attitude of faith and positivity.

Perseverance

Recognizing and remembering that buying your first property will always be the most difficult to hurdle, and keeping an open mind will help you wade through the murky beginnings of the investment process. Developing your mindset and always tying the search back to your 'why' will help you when it feels like there is nothing on the market that fits with your vision. This will help you when you feel like giving up and not continuing along with your dream of real estate investing. Always remember it takes time. Nothing worth having comes quickly. Slow and steady wins the race. The early bird gets the worm, I could keep listing the cliches all day, but it's true; perseverance will win in the end.

But if this isn't your first property, maybe you're now looking for a second or third, perseverance will still be your friend. After the rush of the first property has worn off and you're ready to start building that empire and gaining that passive income, you still need to persevere to find just the right property.

Flexibility

Be prepared to have to change your idea of what you're looking for or where. Maybe you've set your sights on purchasing a single-family home, but there isn't anything in your price range on the market right now, and nothing even in the neighborhood of what you wanted to spend then a condo or townhome in that area in your price range pops up. Do the math. Does it make sense for you to consider this option instead? After all, it could be a great start to your portfolio.

Don't discount something just because it doesn't fit the plan. Be open to other ideas, and stay flexible. Consider the perspective of your future tenant. Maybe it's not something you would live in, but for someone else it could seem like winning the lottery on the size, location, and price. You need this flexibility to accept or consider new properties as they come up and meet your requirements. The worst mistake you could make is being unable to see the opportunities that can start your real estate empire.

Understanding the Basics

- Appreciation. When the house increases in value from the time of purchase and difficult to rely on due to the volatility of the real estate market.
- Cash flow. Purchasing an apartment building to manage and generate a profit from the rental of each unit.
- Real estate income. Brokering sales (buying and selling) and charging a commission or offering to pay a percentage of the sales for managing the property. This could be a property management company, or individual looking after your units. You would pay them a portion of the rent each month to continue day to day operations of the building for you.
- Ancillary real estate investment income. This comes from offering extra services within your building such as laundry services or vending machines. Knowing your clients and their needs, you have the opportunity to start a mini-business within a business.

Identifying Your Comfort Zone

Establish guidelines about what types of property you would like to acquire. Don't just consider everything that comes your way, define what you want your portfolio to look like and what you are willing to pass on.

- How much income do you have?
- How much financing is available to you?
- Which area do you want these properties?

Everyone has a comfort zone with risk. What you need to decide is how much of a chance you are willing to take and how long you are prepared to hold out for the right property. You don't want to say, "A better one will come along, I'll wait." Only to realize you haven't grown financially at all because you were too shy on pulling the trigger. Each time something of interest becomes available, refer to your 'why' column and ask yourself: Does this fit with my vision? Am I holding out for the right property, or am I just being too cautious? Set up the parameters of your comfort zone, so when the time comes, you are better prepared and ready to jump in with an offer.

Treat It Like a Business Not a Hobby

If you haven't already, picture this journey as a business, especially if you are looking to leave your regular job behind. Just like a business, you need a plan of action, and a system in place to accomplish your goals. There will be no success without a plan of action.

Even if you don't plan on leaving your regular job, treating this as a business will mean you are prepared with strategies and boundaries that a hobbyist may not. You don't want to be wondering what made you ever decide to do this on top of your full time job. Have a plan of action whether it's to leave your 9-5 or just have a side project to bring in a bit of extra cash.

Imagine

Start to envision your goals and what you hope to accomplish with your real estate investments. Where do you want your money to take you? Dream BIG! Tie this back to 'why'; everything goes back to that because, without reason, it's easy to get off track. Imagine what it looks and feels like to have those properties generating income. What will you do with that extra income? Try constructing a vision board and place it in a prominent spot you look at every day to remind you of what you are trying to accomplish.

Financial Goals

Determine what it will take for you to reach your financial goals. How much wealth and cash flow do you hope to have? How long will this plan of action take you? What is a realistic timeframe? It may not happen by then, but it will give you something to focus on and work towards. Write these goals down with a specific date.

Vision, Mission, and Values

Most businesses create a vision statement, a mission statement, and consider the values they uphold for themselves and their clients. You should do the same.

A vision statement will keep you on track of the bigger picture. This statement will describe where you want to take your business. Consider this vision statement: Alzheimer's Association: A world without Alzheimer's Disease.

A mission statement supports your vision. If your vision statement is where your company is going, then the mission statement is an action-oriented vision statement. This is declares your what, the who, and the why of your company. Values are what you believe and what you expect others around you to share with you.

As you move through this book, keep all of these in mind as you start your research and due diligence on properties. If a deal doesn't uphold any of these ideals, then you know it probably isn't the right one.

Remember: You don't need to engage in the first or even the second deal you find, nor do you need to pursue every deal that seems halfway good. Based on your vision, mission, and values wait for the right sale. Waiting for the right deal will not only fit in with your values and mission but it will most likely mean that you may have less issues with the property as you did your due diligence and it fit in with your future plans.

Setting SMART Goals

SMART goals are: specific, measurable, achievable, realistic, and time-sensitive. You need to communicate your intentions clearly, hold yourself accountable, draft out the plan, and set milestones.

- Specific. Do you want one property a year? Maybe ten? Do you want to earn an 'x' amount of dollars a month within a specific time frame? Whatever your goal is, you must make it achievable by your standards. There is nothing worse than setting a goal, realizing it's not attainable, and placing it on a shelf to be ignored. That's an illusion, not a goal.
- Measurable. If your goal is too vague, you won't realize when you have "arrived." It will be harder to stick to the plan. Saying you want to be your boss is great, but when? Try setting a very realistic timeline, for example, buying your first property within the next 12 months.
- Attainable. The goal must be realistic if you want to buy your first property within the first year of hunting for a property, is that attainable for you? If not, consider changing the timeline to make it more achievable and motivational. Something to inspire hope and the desire to achieve it.
- Relevant. This is the goal that will spur you into action and challenge your way of thinking. If you have set your sights on purchasing your first property in a year, how can you make this a reality? Maybe

buying a single-family home won't get you to your financial goal as quickly as you would like, but a duplex or fourplex would.
- Time-bound. The goal must be time-bound in that it has to have a start date and end date. It doesn't have to be big, but it needs a time frame for it to occur. Have a date in mind for when you would like to buy your first property. Start prioritizing the things needed to meet that timeline.

Success

To set yourself up for success, you need to consider becoming an expert in one area and knowing it well. These are some ways you can achieve expert status.

- Study the area.
- Read real estate sections in the local newspapers.
- Drive around, get to know the neighborhood.
- Attend open houses.

Stay Positive

Searches can take time. This isn't something that happens overnight and can get discouraging.

Working on your mindset to stay positive will keep you in good spirits even when there is nothing that fits your criteria or a lot of time has passed. Learning to change your thoughts from "I *can't* find the right property" to "I *will* find the right property" will have huge effects on your brain in staying positive throughout the process. Thoughts will suddenly become "I *will* do this" instead of "I *can* do this." Have fun or make a game out of it when possible. Challenge yourself to always find the positive side.

It's been proven that having a successful mindset comes from having a growth mindset instead of a fixed one. Changing how you think and talk about specific things is where this comes in. Just think how saying "I can't" all the time affects our brain. It shuts it down. You stop looking for ideas or ways around things because you've told your mind there is no solution and it doesn't want to work harder than it needs to.

Imagine if you started saying, "How can I?" instead. It puts your brain into overdrive, trying to figure out a new way to make something happen. Whether or not you believe in the Law of Attraction or spirituality, this is what it means to manifest, which can be a powerful tool. Reframing how you talk to yourself and what you envision is all rewiring your brain to believe that anything is possible and will be coming to you.

Start with the end in mind. Where do you want this journey to take you? Then envision how you will get there, how it will feel, then work backward and start using those reframed words. Vision boards, mantras, and affirmations will all assist with this, but the biggest one is flipping any negative thoughts on itself.

- "I can't afford that property" becomes "How can I afford that property?"
- "I can't find a good deal" becomes "How can I find a good deal?"

Do you see the difference? The first one halts brain function, making you more likely to walk away from a potentially great deal or property because you've stopped looking for a solution. In the second phrase, you're thinking in terms of a puzzle, and how can you solve it to make the deal happen? Your brain will automatically move into problem-solving mode. You will start to see solutions, think more creatively, and experience the success you've only seen in movies. Change the way you think, change the way you operate.

Shut out any past failures, missteps, negative thoughts, and any other factors that might prevent you from seeing opportunities along the way. Any negative thoughts are taking up valuable "real estate" in your mind rent-free. Dwelling on what has happened in the past has no bearing on what your future holds. These negative thoughts tend to focus on what has happened in the past and how unsuccessful you may have been, telling you that you can't possibly be successful now, but that has no bearing on what your future will bring.

Do Your Research

Study the area, and get to know the people in and around where you are looking to buy. Network within the local businesses, owners in the area tend to be on-site more often than not, so an introduction can be accessible. Small, non-chain corner stores or coffee shops can have the ear of the locals to know what's going on.

Humans have a natural tendency to want to help those in need. Who do you know that could help you with your endeavor? I'm sure there are hundreds if not thousands of realtors in your area alone, and at least one of them would be willing to take the time to talk to you and answer any questions you are facing.

They say you are the sum of the five people you hang around with the most. So who are you spending the majority of your time with? Do they lift you and support your goals? You should seek out other successful real estate investors to spend some time with. It's good for the soul to meet new people, so why not expand your network of friends to include those who understand your future goals and encourage you to pursue them. No one can tell you what opportunity is right, or when the time is right for you, only you will know that.

See opportunities where others see only problems and become a problem solver. This will help you sharpen your critical thinking skills and measure your tolerance levels. Problems will always arise, but it's how you handle them that will set you apart in the real estate business.

Study, read books, blogs, and forums, listen to podcasts, and watch YouTube videos. No one's too old to study. When searching for blogs or podcasts, start with real estate investing and branch out from there; try wealth building, real estate strategies, investing, passive income, etc.

Blogs:

- Housing Wire
- The BiggerPockets Blog
- CRE Online Blog
- Fundrise Education
- Forbes Real Estate

Podcasts

- Tom Ferry Podcast
- Hack the Entrepreneur
- Kevin & Fred's Next Level Agents Podcast
- The Gary Vee Experience

Consider listening to podcasts or videos on YouTube while driving around. That way you can maximize the time you are spending in your car looking for your next property, while also doing some personal development. When you find a good source of knowledge, ask questions. And lots of them. I was once told that the only stupid question is the one that isn't asked. So ask.

Chapter 3: Understanding Investment Properties

"The road to success and the road to failure are almost exactly the same." - Colin R Davis

As I talk about the inner work required to run your own real estate business, consider what you know and play on your strengths.

Consider an area in your life that you are familiar with that could lend you an edge over your competition when vying for a particular property. Are you ex-military? Consider buying near a base and renting for military transfers as you are familiar with the difficulties military families face when it comes to finding homes in new towns or cities. What would make sense for these families? Having their own home or duplex in a community where they can meet other military families would benefit them and your wallet.

Look into the lifestyle or community that you are familiar with and see what you can leverage in terms of the type of people involved in that same situation. It makes marketing more manageable and you can base your property decisions on this knowledge.

Types of Investment Properties

Single-family Residence

This is the most common type of first investment. There is more available to choose from, all areas have them, and they come in a variety of price ranges.

Pros:

- Easiest to manage
- Fewer bills associated with them
- Better appreciation
- Less expensive to buy
- Easier to finance

Cons:

- They have a higher cost per unit
- It is slower to scale your income/wealth with them
- Expensive to rehab if repairs are needed from the outset

- Potential for more competition
- If the property is too old or in need of too much repair a bank may not lend the money

Multi-family Residence

There are two kinds of multi-family properties: small and large.

Small is considered four units or less, large is considered anything bigger than five. Financing the smaller units is similar to the single-family residence but larger units are treated as commercial property and the rules change significantly, for the sake of this book and these examples I will focus on the smaller multi-family residences.

Pros:

- More cash flow possibilities
- One loan for multiple dwellings
- Multiple units to generate cash flow
- One insurance policy
- Less competition

Cons:

- Expensive to purchase
- Management intensive
- Complicated with a diverse group under one roof
- Fewer to choose from

Condominiums (Condos)

These are individually owned units within a large complex. The owner is responsible for everything within the unit but has shared expenses the Home Owners Association (HOA) look after through a collection of monthly fees from owners. Also, before purchasing consider whether or not the building has a special assessment against it. These assessments are borne by the owners of the units and typically the amount owed is based on the square footage. This value is added to the HOA fees and can eat into your profits.

Another important thing to find out is the rental rules. Some buildings have no restrictions on how many rentals they will allow, others have a percentage of units they will allow to be rented out, and others won't allow rentals. There is a possibility that the allowable rate is already at maximum so you wouldn't be able to rent your unit.

Townhomes

These share many of the same advantages and disadvantages as condos; they are just missing the apartment feel. They tend to be larger with multiple floors, but the HOA still runs the show on what can and can't be done with the units. Some of the upsides of townhomes are they sometimes come with a small piece of green space outdoors to call your own that a condo doesn't have. For some, a nice perk of a townhome is having a garage for your car, a workshop or extra storage. Condos tend to have communal parking and small storage lockers.

Foreclosures

Last, but certainly not least, are foreclosures.

These properties are susceptible to significant issues as they can be left sitting vacant on the market for months, if not years. Problems can present themselves in the way of blatant neglect, mold, foul odor, and vandalism that all require added costs that will have to be dealt with before any renting can occur.

If you have the time and inclination to fix them, you can turn trash into treasure in no time. Investors tend to pass on these opportunities for specific reasons, which means you can save money with your low-ball offer to the bank. As banks are only interested in seeing a return on their otherwise financial loss, they will consider almost any offer. So you shouldn't feel bad about starting at such a low price, they just want it off their books. You can use you leftover cash for necessary renovations and repairs.

Location, Location, Location

What attracts people to a particular neighborhood? What motivates people to move out? What is the turnover in rentals and sales? What is the market for rentals?

These are the questions you want to consider when scoping out locations. Understanding the area you are potentially purchasing in is key to being a successful landlord.

You may hear investors speak about properties being in a Class, for example, Class A, B, C, etc. These classifications aren't standardized, and not every real estate investor uses the same one, so it is not always helpful or accurate way to gauge an area or house. Your version of a Class A location might be someone else's version of Class B and so on. You may come across someone saying, "I have a Class A property in a Class B location." To help you decipher this "code," I have provided some background on Class A, B, and C.

Class A

- Location - This area will have newer buildings, the hottest restaurants, the best schools, and the highest cost real estate. Most likely, the houses and condo buildings will be no more than ten years old. This is the location that most investors want to buy in, and it is the best location where possibly the best tenants are looking to rent.
- Properties - Follows the same concept of generally newer, fewer maintenance issues, modern amenities that all tenants are looking for. They are more in demand, which means a higher purchase price and they will require a higher rent, but because of the higher price, it can translate into smaller cash flow.

Class B

- Location - A little older area than Class A but will still have some decent restaurants, schools, and people. Likely the "middle class" area.
- Properties - Older homes, in the 15 - 30-year range, with some upgrades or renovation needed. Not as in-demand, so a home or apartment building could probably go for a reasonable price. Rental income might be lower, but maintenance could be higher due to the age of the homes and buildings. Again cash flow could be small.

Class C

- Location - Income is much, much lower here. Much older homes and buildings. This Class tends to attract people on social assistance or working minimum wage jobs. Potentially multiple pawn shops and cheque cashing stores in the area.
- Building - These buildings will be much older, approximately 35+ years, and will most likely look it as well. Will probably need numerous and ongoing repairs. Rent

will be low, but the property will be more affordable than the other two Classes.

Other Things to Consider:

Crime/Drugs

Is the area a known hotspot for crime or drugs? You can find out on these websites:

- crimereports.com (Canada and the US)
- city-data.com (the US only)

These are great tools to give you some insight into things like vandalism, petty theft, serious crimes, and the drug trade in the area.

Although drug use can be hard to track and measure, they tend to go hand in hand with the crime levels. If the websites above websites can't help, then ask your neighbors or call the local police department's non-emergency line and ask to speak with someone about the area.

Schools

Most parents will consider the types of schools their kids will be going to before moving into a new area. Any area that is close to a good school will maintain a lower vacancy rate and better tenants than one that is near a school with a bad reputation. Also, the length of tenants staying in an area with good schools will increase if their children are young.

To find out the rating of your local schools check out:

- greatschools.org (the US only)
- Each major city within Canada has a website for schools and their districts. Google the city or town to find out what district it's in. For example, Victoria, BC is District 61, and that website is https://www.sd61.bc.ca/

Jobs & Unemployment Rate

In general, a higher number of jobs make for a stronger rental market but low unemployment rates don't necessarily mean you shouldn't invest there.

Check out various labor sites to get stats before deciding:

- city-data.com (the US only)
- DOL.gov (US Department of Labor)
- Search by Province for Canada

Keep in mind that just because an area has, let's say, a 7% unemployment rate, doesn't mean you shouldn't buy property there. That also means that 93% of the population is gainfully employed. Just be sure to do your due diligence when screening tenants.

Population Growth

While it's hard to predict where an area is seeing growth and where there will be continued growth, an educated guess can be made using the historical data and current trends found on these websites.

- usa.com/rank
- bac-lac.gc.ca (Canada census reports)
- census.gov/construction/nrc (US census)

Use the census to look at housing stats and how many building permits were given out in a specific year. This will also give you an idea of population growth. The more permits submitted, the higher the chance for houses, condos, or townhomes being available for purchase and more future tenants for those properties.

Take a city like Surrey, BC. It has a bad reputation for crime and drug use. In reality, the bad area is one small part of an otherwise thriving city, and many people say they would never live there. While Surrey has one of the worst reputations within the Lower Mainland for crime, it also has one of the largest population growths in the past decade and shows no signs of stopping. From multiple high rises to single-family homes, Surrey is proliferating around its expanding transit system.

Transportation

Considering places with good transit or ease of transport will potentially bring in good tenants as it will make getting to work easier for them, especially in major urban areas where parking may be at a premium. Whether it's a light rapid transit system, a train or city bus, this will increase your chances of finding and maintaining good tenants to keep your property occupied.

Amenities/Trends

An easy way to check out the neighborhoods is by walking them. This way, you will find out what is within walking distance of your property. Parks, gyms, restaurants, theaters, cafes add to the atmosphere of the neighborhood and make it more enticing to prospective renters.

Put these elements together to build a profile of the type of neighborhood you want to buy in and be sure to include the type of tenant you want to rent to. This will make it easier for you when it's time to buy that perfect property and start renting.

Consider this. People used to move out of the city to find a place in the suburbs away for some peace or to raise a family, so housing prices would have been at a premium, especially ones near good schools. Now while these elements are still true today, I think you will find that many people want to be closer to a large community hub due to the increase in gas and food prices among other things. They also want to be closer to work and social events, getting to know neighborhoods and what's available to prospective tenants is key.

Chapter 4: Analyzing a Rental Property

"Don't let the fear of losing be greater than the excitement of winning." - Robert Kiyosaki

Cash flow and appreciation are the two things you should look at when analyzing properties. To put it plainly, cash flow is the money left over after the bills have been paid. Appreciation is the equity built up as the property value increases. Now, it's not a good idea to rely on appreciation as the market ebbs and flows as there is no guarantee that your property will appreciate.

Income - Expenses = Cash Flow

Your cash flow is what will determine if the property is right for you. This is what you calculate to see what capital is left at the end of the month after everything has been paid out.

Where people tend to get a little mixed up and start to make errors is combining income with expenses or assume something is an expense when it may not be or not calculating enough for expenses. I will go into income and expenses in greater detail below.

Speculating

According to the Cambridge English Dictionary, the term speculating is defined as "to guess possible answers to a question when you do not have enough information to be certain."

So to extend that to the real estate market, speculating means assuming the property will increase in value and that you can cover the costs, which can be stressful, given the volatility of the market.

In the 80s and 90s, speculation was a big part of real estate because leveraging had a bad rap, and the market was on the upward swing. You almost couldn't lose even if you weren't entirely sure of your expenses or the income generated. However, now, in the volatile market we are in now, can you afford to speculate?

There is little need for this guesswork as more technology has become available in the form of apps that can calculate mortgage costs, expenses, and help you plan to cover them in their entirety. The biggest reason for beginners being unsuccessful in this venture is underestimating their costs. The renter covers some, but what's left are capital expenditures and will be paid by you over the life of ownership. These expenses include roof repairs or replacement, hot water tanks, appliances, plumbing, and electrical issues, and/or new windows. You can't always plan for them, but you can prepare yourself and pad your wallet ahead of time.

Return on Investment (ROI)

Return on Investment or ROI is defined by Merriam Webster's Dictionary as "measuring the gain or loss generated on investment to the amount of money invested." This is the most widely used way of determining profitability because of its flexibility to determine the percentage of invested money that is recouped after associated costs/expenses are deducted. Because of its versatility, you should know that ROI's numbers can sometimes be manipulated to suit the person calculating them.

ROI = profit/cost x 100

While this equation may seem straightforward, it leaves out other variables you should take into consideration with real estate. Such as the amount financed from the bank for the initial investment, repairs, maintenance, advertising, and appraisals. All of these can affect the ROI numbers.

In general, ROI will be higher if the cost of the purchase is lower. It's good to shop around for terms of investments as the financing can significantly impact the price of the investment, which in turn will affect your ROI.

The Cost Method

The cost method calculates ROI by dividing the equity in the property by the property's cost. It requires the dividing of the equity position by all the costs related to the purchase and repairs of the property.

You buy a property for $500,000 and need to put in $25,000 repairs and maintenance. After the work is completed, the property is now valued at $650,000. The difference is $125,000. $125,000/$650,000 x 100 = 0.192 or 19%.

Other things can complicate the ROI figure, such as refinancing or taking out a second mortgage because of changing interest rates. The loan amount may increase, and so will the associated fees.

The Out-Of-Pocket Method

This is a preferred method by real estate investors because of the higher return. Using the same numbers as above, but instead of paying for it upfront, you purchase with financing and a down payment of $100,000. Therefore, the initial out of pocket expense is $100,000 plus the $25,000 for repairs and maintenance, which makes your total out of pocket expenses $125,000. The new value of the property stays the same at $650,000, which now makes the equity $525,00. So $525,000/$650,000 = 0.80 or 80%.

This is what it means to leverage a property because the ROI more than doubles.

However, even knowing all this, the investment can not truly be valued until the property sells. Even then, it doesn't always equal profit because there will be times when a property does not sell for market value.

What Is Income?

This is the fair market value of what you can charge for rent. This is based on location, type of property, how many bedrooms and bathrooms, what kinds of amenities there are, and the size of the property, etc.

All of this will help determine what you charge for the property or unit. This isn't to say you add everything up that you will be out of pocket for and charge that amount to recoup your costs. This means checking out what the market will bear for a current rental price. You don't want to undervalue the unit or property, as you run the risk of finding tenants that don't value it the same as you, and overvaluing the property runs the risk of it remaining vacant.

Check out your local papers, Craigslist, or any other social sites that offer rental listings. Look at competitor's websites or property management company websites to see what they have listed. If you know other landlords in your area, talk to them. If you have a lot of applicants, this is an opportunity to consider the market and raise rental prices.

What Is an Expense?

These are the out of pocket expenses that go into owning and running a property. For example, let's say you purchased a house, and your mortgage was $800/month. You decide that the market will bear you charging $1000/month, so you believe that you have a cash flow of $200/month. That would be false. You haven't taken into consideration any of the expenses listed below.

- Property taxes
- Insurance
- Vacancies
- Repairs
- Capital expenditures
- Water
- Sewer
- Garbage pickup
- Recycling
- Gas
- Electricity
- Homeowners Association
- Strata Fees (Canada)
- Snow removal (if applicable)
- Lawn maintenance
- Property management

- Flood insurance
- Earthquake insurance

Some of these will be easy to calculate as you can call the city and find out about property taxes for your location. Still, some will not be as easy to calculate, not all will apply to every type of property, and in some cases, the tenant will pay for the expenses as the rent will cover it.

It can get tricky when accounting for the vacant rates, capital expenditures, repairs, and a property management company (if you use one). Try to average them out, so when something happens, you're not thrown off. Maintaining good records will help with tracking and calculating your various expenses so that over the years will be able to average your costs better. Whether you are you doing this yourself or have an accountant managing it for you, the better records you keep, the easier it will be during tax time. There are also apps that I have listed in the additional resources chapter that go into various property management and accounting apps that can assist with calculating these expenses.

Vacancy Rates

While it's impossible to estimate how many units might be vacant at any given time, you will need to understand that at some point, it will happen. Now, how long they stay empty will depend on your area and how good you are at advertising your available units. If you think it could be for longer than a month or two months, you need to add the expense into your calculation, so you're not out of pocket for those months the unit is empty.

For starters, you can talk to any local property management company if you don't have one and find out what they average for vacancy rates. Once you know what the typical vacancy rate is, as a percentage, you can start to break it down. Let's say you charge $1000/month for rent. You have found out that the vacancy rate is approximately 5%. You will divide $1000 by 5% or 0.05 to get $50. This is what you will want to set aside in your vacancy rate contingency fund.

Repairs

Repairs can be tough to estimate. A single-family home built in 1944 will need more repairs than a home under 20 years ago. A recently rehabbed building will require less regular maintenance than an apartment building neglected by owners for many years. Similarly, we can never estimate how much we will need for a random vehicle repair other than routine maintenance required once a year; the same can be said for a rental property. If you're anything like me, you set aside money for your vehicle as it is essential to your quality of life, so you should also have savings specifically for your property. A general rule of thumb for vehicle repairs is approximately $150/month, so translating that to property repairs it is 5% - 15% depending on the age of the building. Keep in mind this is an average; every building is different. You may find that you go months without any repairs, but then you may need to unexpectedly replace the water tank because of a burst or leak. You will have already planned for this, so you won't take the hit.

Capital Expenditures

These are the "big" ticket items that you can't always plan for but know you will need to deal with at some point over the life of your ownership. They don't need to be replaced often, but when they do, they typically cost a fair amount. Things such as roof repair or replacement, appliances, plumbing, electrical systems, windows, driveways, etc.

These can be hard to budget for because a lot of it will depend on the age of the building or house you purchase as well as the age of expenditures at the time of purchase.

Capital Expense	Total Replacement	Cost Lifespan (years)	Cost per Year	Cost per Month
Roof	$10,000	25	$400	$33.33
Water Heater	$1000	10	$100	$8.33
All Appliances	$2,000	10	$200	$16.66
Driveway/Parking Lot	$5,000	50	$100	$8.33
HVAC	$3,000	20	$150	$12.50
Flooring	$2,000	6	$333	$27.75
Plumbing	$3,000	30	$100	$8.33

			0	
Windows	$5,000	50	$100	$8.33
Paint	$2,500	5	$500	$41.67
Cabinets/Counters	$5,000	20	$250	$20.83
Structure (foundation, framing)	$10,000	50	$200	$16.67
Components (garage, door, etc.)	$1,000	10	$100	$8.33
Landscaping	$1,000	10	$100	$8.33
TOTAL	**$50,500**		**$2,633**	**$219.42**

Figure 1 - Examples of Capital Expenditures. Adapted from *The Book on Rental Property Investing: How to Create Wealth and Passive Income Through Intelligent Buy & Hold Real Estate Investing!* B. Turner Copyright © 2015 by BiggerPockets Inc.

This table shows the replacement cost, the lifespan for the top 13 capital expenditures, and what should be budgeted for the month to make sure it's covered. The other part of this table is that it assumes all the expenditures are brand new, but each one will most likely be at a different stage in its lifecycle. Keep in mind these are fictional numbers for an average property that doesn't exist. So while this will give you an idea of what a capital expenditure is and what they can cost, it pays to do your due diligence in your area to see what these associated costs will be and work on a budget that way.

What Makes a "Good" Rental Property?

I believe this is a highly subjective topic as each investor will have their own ideas of what makes a property "good" outside of the potential to earn decent cash flow. There is no "perfect" property, just one that helps you achieve your financial goals. So given all the information above about expenses and income, what does it take to have a suitable property?

Attributes

These are going to be the things that prospective tenants are looking for in a home, and you want to consider to bring in the steady, stable, long term tenants you are looking for.

Enough bedrooms. I recommend at least three per house. Two is standard depending on the area but if your tenants are a young couple looking to build a family, then they will soon run out of space, and you will be looking for new tenants before you know it. Any more, and you will need to target a specific market of a tenant with either a large family or is wealthy. If you are targeting a large home with plans to fill it with a family also consider this, kids are naturally hard on posessions. Appliances, carpets, and walls will take a beating and need replacing sooner than a smaller family in a smaller home. The average family size in the US, as of 2018, is 2.5 and on the rise. Sticking to three or four bedrooms keeps the family unit small-ish and with enough room to grow. This will keep down the wear and tear of the house and appliances. Three bedrooms are also easier to resell down the road.

The age of the house. Older homes are less expensive upfront, but the cost comes later with pricey repairs, as they could be less energy efficient due to older windows or the house may have settled, so the door jambs don't meet. Because of this, you want to be aware that tenants may not be happy about higher heating bills, which could make it harder to rent out. Newer homes, of course, have a higher purchase price but require less maintenance with fewer issues needing repair in the long term.

Renters like the option for extra storage. By the time they are old enough to venture out on their own they have accumulated a lot of baggage. So looking for a garage is a good idea as that will provide your tenants with a place to store their car or sporting gear or whatever else it is that they need to store away. Having a garage will only add to the appeal of your listing.

Utility price. It's a good strategy to require the tenant to pay these. Personal habits or "creature comforts" vary, so there is always the chance of the electric bill skyrocketing in the summer by leaving all of the windows open with the A/C running 24 hours a day. And the same for the gas bill going up in winter. While there are tenants who will be careful and honest about the bills you don't want to risk it, make sure they know what you cover and anything else is their responsibility.

An outdoor area. While having outside space to relax and enjoy can be a big selling point, I wouldn't recommend a large sprawling yard with expensive lawn decor or delicate plants for your properties, unless you plan to implement a maintenance system that you pay for. The reality is, it may look very nice to buyers and future tenants, but don't expect upkeep by your renter. If you can find something with a small outdoor space such as a patio or side yard, then you've hit the jackpot. A recreational space is essential, so if your prospective property doesn't have one I would recommend making sure it's at least close to a park and mention it in your property rundown.

Parking. Always a plus to have space for your tenants to park at least one car, whether it's a driveway, carport, or garage. It's better than street parking with growing traffic congestion, especially in the city, tenants might not be willing to risk damage to their vehicles.

These are just a few of the things I would consider when looking to invest in a rental property. You may have other attributes on your list, and that's good. Just make sure it's something that would bring value to your purchase and you know is something that a prospective tenant wants.

Problems to Consider

First, try not to see them as problems, but challenges instead. It's all about morphing how you look at what you own and what they can do for you in terms of cash flow. Most of the "problems" listed below others may walk away from as they are considered too difficult or not worth the trouble. This can make it easier for you to get a better deal on the property. Don't forget to include these repairs in your budget as they will increase the value of the property. Pricing out new or unfamiliar repairs may seem like a daunting task, so here is some clarity on those tough projects.

- Old house stench. That smell that tells you as soon as you open the door that this house is old, musty or something died here. Usually, it's one of four things, pet urine in the carpets, cigarette smoke, sewage, or mildew. You can figure it out by process of elimination and some deep cleaning. It's good to rule out if the smell is coming from within the walls, where rodents may have had a nest and then died. Then you will need to bring in a professional.

- Old carpets. You can try steam cleaning it yourself, but it's easier to have the carpets and underlay replaced as you are required to do as a landlord.
- Stained tile. Clean all the laminate or tile floors thoroughly in the kitchen and bathroom(s) with a heavy solution of bleach and water. Open all windows and let the property air out for a few days to get rid of the bleach smell. Once the bleach smell is gone you will know if there is still an odor.
- Cleaning. Do a top to bottom cleaning of the entire house. I would recommend hiring a cleaner to do the job for you. If you decide to do it yourself, start with washing the walls, even if they don't look dirty at first glance. You will see all the dirt and grime melt away, especially if the previous owners were smokers. Use warm soapy water and a 50/50 bleach solution for the tougher areas.
- Painting. After the walls are clean, patch up any holes or dings and make sure to use a primer, such as Kilz Primer, to eliminate

any lingering odors. Apply a fresh coat of paint, and your room will look brand new.
- Out of date kitchen. Have you seen the Harvest Gold appliances from that decade? If not, Google it. While most of them are no longer in use, some may have survived unnoticed. While replacing appliances isn't cheap, but they are an easy fix. Painting old dark cupboards and replacing the hardware is less than a day's work, low cost, and will dramatically improve the look of your interior. New counter-tops can be purchased prefab from stores like Home Depot and Lowe's for just a few hundred dollars.
- Bad roof. This is a red flag for would-be investors but can make negotiating a deal easy. While having a leaky, cracked, or old roof may sound daunting and can get expensive, you can shop around for deals. Plus, a brand new roof adds to the resale value.
- Mold. Mold can be a death sentence for infrastructure if you let it go for too long. It can hide inside walls, smell terrible, and cause problems for people with asthma or compromised immune systems. Mold appears when there is an excess of

moisture, so if you can pinpoint, fix, and clean up the moisture problem, it's not so scary. Try using a special solution, such as Aegis Microbe Shield, designed specifically to get rid of mold but must be administered by a professional. If it comes back, it's a good idea to get the entire house checked.

- Overgrown Yards. Curb appeal is huge in real estate. If the yard looks like a tangled jungle of a mess, it won't be appealing to prospective tenants who may worry they have to clean it up. It doesn't take much to clear out weeds, trim hedges and trees, and mow the lawn to make it rental ready. It's not expensive and will change the whole look of the house once it's completed.

Note: Anything to do with the foundation can turn a house or property into a money pit. From cracks to water leaks, these can be severely problematic. I'm not saying dismiss them completely, but be aware that if you do, it could be the root of other major problems, and that equates to more time, energy, and cash which will eat into your cash flow.

Financial Considerations

Once you have chosen your property, it's time to examine the financial considerations, such as income, expenses, and debt. This requires a fair amount of paperwork and calculations, but a bit of time upfront will help make the decision easier and run less risk of making the wrong decision about the property.

- Gross scheduled income - This is what you would collect if all units were rented.
- Vacancy & credit loss - What is not rented and any non-payment from tenants.
- Gross operating income - This is the amount you expect to collect and have available to pay operating expenses after deducting your vacancy and credit loss.
- Operating expenses - Necessities to keep the lights on and income flowing. However, if you stick with a single-family home or condo unit, these expenses would be borne by the tenant and not you. In an apartment building, the tenant would pay some of these expenses, but you would pay a portion as well.

Subtract expenses from the gross operating income gives you the net operating income. This is the income before financing or income taxes and after vacancy and expenses.

Another factor to consider is the Capitalization Rate (Cap Rate), which is the most common way to assess profitability and return potential. This represents what a property will yield over a one-year time frame. However, this is assumed on an unleveraged property, one that is purchased upfront with all cash. The simplest formula is:

Cap Rate = Net Operating Income/Current Market Value

- Net Operating (expected) Annual Income, minus all expenses
- Market Value (present-day value of the asset as per market rates)

For example: if you have $500,000 to invest in a condo. Assume the total rent for the year is $30,000 with maybe $2,500 for repairs over the year.

$30,000 - $2,500 = $27,500

$27,500/$500,000 = 5.5% Cap Rate

Various things can affect the cap rate and change it significantly over the years. Real estate is risky, but the return can be worth it.

Now as with anything in real estate there are going to be risk factors. These could include:

- Age, location, and status of the property - less desirable properties which are most likely in less desirable locations will keep your cap rate higher than a more desirable property or location
- Regular rentals versus vacancy - having regular tenants that stay and pay on time will produce a higher cap rate than regular vacancies
- Property type
- Overall market rate of the property - the closer you get to the core of any major metropolis city, home and commercial prices will generally be higher which will produce lower cap rates

One way to keep the cap rate high is to buy in low-income areas. I know this may put the property in a lower class than I suggested buying in before, but it is one way to start your portfolio for less than expected and get the cap rate high for resale. Properties that you can purchase for cheap and revamp will appreciate. Low cap rates mean less risk and buying newer properties that don't require any work could see a lower return. So based on the Classes listed above and now knowing what the cap rate means you will need to decide how you want to proceed with which kind of property and what kind of area you want to purchase in.

Chapter 5: Tax Implications

"There are no secrets to success. It is the result of preparation, hard work, and learning from failure." - Colin Powell

There are two major markets that I will focus on for this chapter; the United States and Canada. They are similar in some ways, and I have broken down the differences into two sections. Make sure to check with an accountant or financial advisor to make sure you fully understand everything involved with keeping track of financial records for your taxes.

United States

All income from a rental property must be reported. In general, all the associated expenses can be deducted. Again, always check with a financial expert when considering any deductions.

There are two types of taxes you can operate under:

- Cash basis taxpayer - Reports rental income for the year you receive it, regardless of when it was earned. Deduct expenses in the year you paid them.
- Accrual method - Report income when you earn it, rather than after you receive it and deduct the expenses when they are incurred, rather than when you paid them.

Income

You must include all gross income amounts you receive as rent. In addition to regular rent payments, there are other forms of rent considered by the IRS that must be included, as well.

- Advance rent - Any amount received before the period it covers; include it in the year you receive it regardless of the period it covers. For example, your tenant signs a one year lease, but you ask for first and last month's rent upfront, so they pay you $800 for the first month and $800 for the last month. You must include $1600 in the first taxation year.
- Security deposits - Another form of advance rent. Only include this on your income if you don't plan on returning the

deposit when the tenant leaves. If you do plan on returning a portion of the deposit, then you must claim the remaining value as income.

- Canceling a lease - Payment for canceling a lease is considered rent, as the tenant is required to pay you to get out of a lease agreement. This needs to be included as income in the year you received it.
- Expenses paid by a tenant - If a tenant pays any of your expenses, these are included as rent.
- Property or services - If you receive any services from a tenant in lieu of rent, then you need to record the amount they would have paid you as rent as income. For example, if your tenant is a painter or plumber and offers to paint the property or fix any plumbing issues in exchange for no rent for two months, then you need to include the two months rent amount as income.

Expenses

Various expenses that can be deducted from the income generated from the rental properties.

- Mortgage interest

- Property tax
- Operating expenses
- Depreciation
- Repairs
- Advertising
- Maintenance
- Utilities
- Insurance

Note: Specific materials and supplies to keep the property in working order can be entered as maintenance. However, you may not include the costs associated with improvements as these are covered under depreciation.

Canada

As with the US, you must declare all rental income, the only caveat to that would be if you decide to rent to a friend or family member for less than the fair market value of the unit. However, then you also can't claim any expenses spent on that unit.

Expenses

The most common expenses in Canada to claim are:

- Capital - this would be higher costs like a new roof or furnace.
- Current - these are small expenses such as new building paint or driveway repair.

Other expenses include:

- Heat
- Hydro
- Water
- Advertising
- Legal fees
- Accounting
- Utilities
- Maintenance
- Property taxes
- Administration fees
- Office expenses
- Wages

You may also be able to claim the depreciable property. However, you can not claim land, only the building that is on the land. As long as you are renting out at fair market value, then you can claim the full amount of the expenses above.

Canada has different classes that properties fall into, so be aware of where your property may fall before claiming any expenses.

- Condos, for example, are considered a Class 1.
- Leasehold interest can be claimed as Class 1, 3, 6, or 13.
- Class 13 is the capital cost of the leasehold interest.
    - The tenant make capital improvements or alterations
    - Money spent by the tenant to obtain or renew the lease

You can not claim the expense when the tenant pays to cancel the contract, but you do need to include the money as income from the cancellation.

Claims you can't make:

- Land transfer tax
- Mortgage principal
- Personal labor costs for repairs

While doing this research, I found that you could claim home insurance and mortgage interest, but when I dug further, I also found instances saying you can't claim these things. So I strongly recommend verifying these expenses with an accountant before claiming either.

Capital Cost Allowance

There is an option to claim what is called Capital Cost Allowance (CCA) on major renovations, such as replacing windows. This is used to claim for depreciation, but it also means that you pay capital gains when you sell the property.

Another option is not to claim the CCA, but you aren't able to depreciate major renovations. An upside to claiming the CCA is that you don't pay capital gains when you sell the property. I would advise talking to a financial professional regarding your options and why one would be better than the other.

If you decide to claim the CCA, then there are items you can write off such as the capital cost of the property, and various other items, I would consult an accountant to see what else can be claimed.

Because real estate typically appreciates, instead of depreciating, any claims made may have to be included back into income after the property is sold. Selling can result in a recapture of your CCA if, upon selling the property, it is found that the proceeds of the sale exceed the undepreciated capital cost amount.

Pros and Cons of CCA

- Pros - lowers your taxable income
- Cons - when you sell, all the CCA claims are recaptured and treated as taxable income

Now that we've covered the boring tax stuff that is necessary, let's talk about something a little more fun, financing the property. In the next chapter, I'll go over the different ways you can go about funding your property, and I'll be giving you some creative ways to go about this as well as the tried and true.

See you on the other side.

Chapter 6: Financing Investment Properties

"Successful people do what unsuccessful people are not willing to do. Don't wish it were easier, wish you were better." - Jim Rohn

Whether you are independently wealthy, have a lot in savings or simply plan to have a mortgage for each property, you need to decide how you are going to purchase your properties. I will cover a few of the different ways that you can go the route of financing if you don't have enough cash at the beginning.

Leveraging vs. All Cash

Leveraging is using other people's money to make more money for you. Instead of paying out of pocket for them, it will free up cash for you to do other things or save for future repairs and maintenance. In the US, most conventional lenders will issue a mortgage and then bundle it up and sell that loan package to one of two government sponsored entities Federal National Mortgage Association (FNMA, or Fannie Mae) and the Federal Home Loan Mortgage Corporation (FHLMC, or Freddie Mac). The reason for this is so that the lender can free up their money to re-loan to others. As with any other mortgage lender these two entities will have their own loan amount ranges and borrower score credit minimums among other things.

Within Canada you would typically just go through a mortgage broker to get the best rate deal or straight to a bank or credit union. There isn't a lot of competition between the lenders as the rates are set by the Bank of Canada. I believe a the time of purchasing my condominium in 2009 the rate difference between a couple of the lenders was 0.25%.

There are things to consider when leveraging:

- 15 or 30-year mortgages
- Fixed interest rate or variable

Always try to put enough money down to keep the cash flow positive. This accounts for margins of error if something unexpected occurs. Also, be prepared for more money down and a higher interest rate as it's not your primary residence.

Shop around for the best rates. Places like LendingTree will compete for your business, so you get an excellent deal. Don't forget to be open and assert negotiation. Even knocking 0.5% off the interest rate will save you big dollars in the long run.

Consider this. If you own stocks, it's 100% of your money, and you control 100% of that investment, but in real estate with leveraging, you pay around 20% of your money to control 100% of a property. Who doesn't want that? When you sell, hopefully, your returns have multiplied because you were making money each month on the full value of the investment.

Look at it this way. Two people both have $100,000 to invest in real estate. Person A decides to buy one piece of property for $100,000 in case outright. After expenses, the property generates $500/month in cash flow. At the end of one year, they will have made $6,000 or 6% ROI. Person B invests $20,000 into five different properties. After expenses are paid, the properties generate a $200/month positive cash flow per house. At the end of one year, they will have made $12,000 or a 12% ROI. Person B not only makes more money than Person A, but they control more real estate, approx, $500,000 worth compared to $100,000. Diversification is better in the long run.

Now, there are generally two camps of people, the ones who leverage and the ones who believe in only using cash. As the example above shows, leveraging does provide a better ROI, but there is also something to be said for "no debt," as long as you can carry the costs if the property remains vacant for any amount of time.

All cash is the easiest way to complete the transaction as there are typically fewer complications. Still, the reality is that for most investors, especially first-time investors, all cash isn't going to be an option.

Pros for Leveraging

- Low-interest rates - help keep mortgage payment low and maximizes cash flow.
- Longer terms - up to 30 years for a mortgage repayment, which helps keep payments low.

Cons for Leveraging

- Loan amount maximum - a bank will never lend out more than ten loans to one person in the US, but even getting that many

could be tough due to debt-to-income ratio.
- Slow process - loans are not fast to obtain and can take 30 days or more to secure.
- Property condition - banks tend to only loan money out on properties that are in good shape, sometimes ruling out "fixer uppers."
- Not entity friendly - banks don't like loaning money to LLC's.
- Market drops - the real estate market can be volatile, and the value could drop. If there is a steady decline in the equity, then you could end up owing more than the house is worth, which eliminates any profits made.

Pros for All Cash

- Easy to buy and sell - it's easier to negotiate with cash in hand. It cuts out any need for a bank that could otherwise affect your credit rating and whether you get a reasonable interest rate.
- No mortgage - extra money you would have typically spent on a mortgage can be diverted into repairs, savings, travel, or other investments.

- Sense of security - if you lose your job, you wouldn't have to worry about the bank foreclosing on your property.
- Available equity - you can tap the equity in times of hardship by getting a home equity loan, which is like taking out a second mortgage on your home. This involves refinancing your house for a larger amount and getting the balance in cash. A home equity credit line is similar to a credit card where you have available cash to take out if needed. However, you never want to use either option as an ATM; it can severely ruin your credit.

Cons for All Cash

- Loss of liquidity - cash tied up in real estate is not easily accessed except through a sale, so it should only be considered if you have a comfortable cushion of cash for emergencies.
- Lack of leverage - debt in real estate is not a bad thing; it can be a good thing because the more leveraged you are, the harder it is for someone to consider suing you. Think of it this way, if you don't have any debt against your property and a tenant slips and falls and feels it's your fault because

maybe the stairs were icy, they then hire a lawyer to sue you for negligence. They can sue for your property appreciation amount or more. But if you are fully leveraged on your property, there is no equity to touch, and a lawyer is unlikely to take the case.
- No tax advantage - buying a home with cash offers no tax deductions.

Portfolio Lenders

Unlike conventional lenders, some banks within the United States choose to hold onto their loans and keep the money within the community. These are typically called portfolio lenders. They don't always play by government rules, and this 'allows' them to be a little more creative with their lending. That doesn't mean it's any easier to get a loan here; there are still qualifications that need to be met with approval. What it could mean, however, is flexibility, and by building a relationship with one or more of these lenders, you may be able to avoid the ten loan maximum. Caution: this leniency can also be met with stricter terms of above-average credit ratings and non-negotiable money down.

These portfolio lenders aren't everywhere. You have to search for them, focus on small community banks or credit unions that have less than 20 branches. You will have to ask if they offer these services as they are not usually listed. But beware of balloon payment requirements. At the 10-year mark of a 30-year loan, they may expect a large "balloon" payment, usually done through refinancing.

Private Lenders

It could be a friend, family member, or a person who is looking to invest in the real estate market short-term. Sometimes they want to invest longer-term opportunities if you happen to find one of these people hang on to them and treat them well. They don't come around often.

Typically they will charge between 6-12% interest on the loan. Consider offering on the higher side once you find someone who is willing to do this for you. Yes, that is higher than a bank, but there are a lot fewer hoops to jump through. It makes sense to consider private lending when wanting to purchase an older home that is not move-in ready, and the banks don't want to work with you.

Private lending allows for more time to fix up the property and get it rentable while paying them the mortgage. Once it's ready to rent out, you have a better chance with the bank to get a long term loan at a lower interest rate, so you pay back the private lender any additional money owed.

You might wonder why would anyone hurry to pay back a lender instead of pocketing all the money. As a lender, they will receive a promissory note from you agreeing to pay back the money, and put a lien against the property through the title company or lawyer. This stands until they receive their full payment, so if you don't hold up your end of the bargain they can claim the house through foreclosure. They should also consider being on any insurance you have like title insurance and hazard insurance, depending on your state's requirements.

So, how do you go about finding a private lender? Mention you're looking to invest in polite conversation with new acquaintances. You never know when you could be talking to someone interested in getting involved. If you don't, how will anyone know? This includes posting about it on social media.

Ask your competition. You will find that some real estate investors want to invest in other deals because of the opportunity to turn a profit without putting in the work is gratifying. Second, you need to have a perfect deal; otherwise, how can you pitch the lender? You need to be able to bring something to the table for them to see, so they know they will be getting a profit. The most important part is the pitch. It may be intimidating, but it helps to have a short, simple presentation ready to go.

Getting Creative

Home Equity

If you own your own home, you might be able to use some of the equity to purchase your rental property.

The spread between what is owed on your home and what it's valued at is what can be borrowed. Home equity loans or lines of credit have very low-interest rates. While they are similar, they do have some differences.

The home equity loan is based on what your house is worth and what is left owing on the mortgage. You can then take out the balance for whatever repairs or renovations are needed or as a down payment on a new piece of property. The home equity loan is typically taken out all at once and paid back in monthly installments, as you would a car loan or mortgage.

Same as a home equity loan, the home equity credit line is the balance between what the house is worth and what is left owing. But in this case it is a revolving account that can be used as you need it. You borrow as much or as little as you need, up to the limit, pay back the minimum interest payment, and then borrowing again. Credit lines generally have the lowest interest rates.

Partnerships

These can be a valuable tool for real estate as two or more people can work together to cover or counter each other's shortcomings. Knowing your weaknesses in a business can help you find a partner who excels doing the things you're not good at and can take the pressure off of tasks that you don't enjoy doing.

Never pick someone based on convenience. This is an important decision, take the same care with this that you would take in choosing a spouse.

Choose carefully and with great consideration, maybe because they would be fun to work with or they have something you lack, and vice versa. Make sure your goals and work ethic are compatible, then have a lawyer draw up an agreement to protect you both.

House Hacking

Finally, there is house hacking. For those of you just starting on a real estate journey or not sure if being a landlord is for them, this could be one of the best ways to get started and finance your deal and see what it means to be a landlord.

House hacking refers to combining your primary residence with an investment. You can accomplish this one of two ways:

- A live-in flip - you buy an older, single-family home to fix it up and resell within a couple of years. You complete the renovations while making it your primary residence.
- A small, multi-family property - usually a two- to four-family unit; you live in one unit and rent out the others.

This can be a smart option because of the relatively easy financing given to homeowners, and since it will be your primary residence, you can apply for the homeowner's grant at tax time. Consider it this way, you find a duplex or triplex you like, with a Federal Housing Administration (FHA) loan, and you are only required to put down around 3.5% down. On a $200,000 property, that is just $7,000, plus closing costs. Depending on the market value at the time, you could potentially live mortgage-free until it's time to buy your next property.

Just keep in mind that you can only have one FHA loan at a time. So if this is something you would like to continue doing, you will have to consider refinancing the original property to a different loan or mortgage before moving on to the next property.

There are other benefits to house hacking, such as great cash flow because, in the case of buying a small multi-family building, the likelihood is the tenants will be paying your mortgage payment and splitting some of the other bills, while you live rent-free or almost rent-free.

Going this route, it is also a fairly low-risk way to introduce yourself to the world of being a landlord. Yes, you will be onsite, so they may contact you more than if you lived off-site, but then you will start to understand boundaries and how important they will be now and in the future, as your portfolio grows.

As with other properties, do your due diligence. A bad deal could wind up costing you more, and then you may as well continue only renting. Do your homework, shop around. It may not be the secret to success, but house hacking can be a powerful tool to start building your financial freedom.

Once you have decided which route is best for you and your finances, it's time to get pre-approved. It makes sense to do this before any deals come up, that way you will know ahead of time which property to start the offer process on and which one you have to walk away from because it's out of your price range. Don't let this dissuade you as prices are always negotiable. Now you're ready to start making offers.

Chapter 7: Making an Offer

You have found the perfect property, and now you want to make an offer. You can do this with the help of a real estate agent whose job is to walk you through the whole process. This section will take you through the different ways to go about searching out listings and what to consider when making an offer.

Through Multiple Listing Service (MLS) Listings

Most likely if you're looking through an MLS Listing then you have a real estate agent, if not you can use the same agent on the listing but be mindful of a potential conflict of interest. The listing agent is morally obligated to get the seller the best price but is also working to get you the best price. Some states have made this practice illegal, so check before agreeing to go with the same agent. Up until as recently as 2018 in British Columbia, dual agency (one realtor for both seller and buyer) was common practice but now the Province is working to limit this. However, other Provinces have not banned the use of dual agency yet. Check all the boxes, sign on the dotted lines, and send an offer to the seller. Once the offer is sent off, then you have to wait for a response.

Offering on a Property Not Listed on MLS

If the property is not listed, you may not need a real estate agent, as this is a much less formal way to make an offer. For your first property purchase I wouldn't recommend going this route but it can be done. However if this isn't your first property purchase this can be a much faster way to obtain property and cheaper due to less fees paid out.

On a far less official route you will most likely tour a property and find out how much the seller is asking. You will need to do your research and chat with the owner about the features and amenities then after some negotiation you should arrive at a price. Then you would pull out your official purchase and sale document, both of you would sign it to make it official.

It's just good business to have a lawyer look over any legally binding documents to make sure nothing was missed.

Earnest Money Deposit

This is a good faith deposit and with this you are telling the seller that you are serious about purchasing. Should you not keep up your end of the contract, the seller keeps the money. There are, however, some conditions that allow you to back out of the contract without losing the money and these will be covered later. The amount depends mainly on the price of the property, and although there are no hard and fast rules around this, the deposit tends to be 1% - 2% of the purchase price. Usually held by a third party, most likely the title company or attorney who is handling the closing.

What exactly is this money used for? There are three possible scenarios that could play out, depending on how the deal is done.

- If the sale goes through, the earnest money becomes part of the cash the buyer would be required to bring to closing.
- If the sale does not go through, but the buyer has a legal reason to back out, the deposit is returned.
- If the sale does not go through, and the buyer does *not* have a legal reason the deposit is forfeited to the seller.

So what are some "legal reasons" for backing out of the contract?

Most contracts will contain specific provisions that outline conditions or "contingencies" in which the agreement could be terminated. In other words, the property sale is contingent on some individually listed things within the contract. These are loopholes that will allow you to not follow through on your contract, should one of those contingencies happen to occur. So just what kind of contingencies should you put into your offer?

Be cautious to not put too many contingencies into your contract as that will make the seller leery of accepting your offer. That's not to say don't put any contingencies in. These will protect you from things that you couldn't necessarily anticipate, be careful about how many you put in as you don't want to appear nit picky or just looking for a reason to get out of the contract.

The two most common contingencies to put in are:

- Inspection - generally speaking, you want to have an inspector to look at the property and make sure of no surprises. We'll go over this more in-depth in the next

chapter. A lot of real estate investors will waive this contingency in favor of not letting it stand in the way of a sale. It boils down to personal preference and your comfort level with risk.
- Financing - This contingency allows the buyer to back out and get their deposit back if financing falls through. However, if you are paying cash for the property then you don't need this contingency in the contract.

What Should Your Offer Include?

This could be summed up in six simple words: who, what, when, where, why, and how.

- WHO is making the offer and to WHOM? State who you are and who will be making the offer to
- WHAT is being bought and for WHAT amount? What kind of property is the deal being made on and how much you are offering
- WHERE am I getting the funds? Where the funding will be coming from (bank loan or cash)

- WHEN am I planning to buy it? (the closing date)
- WHY would I back out of this offer? (the contingencies)
- HOW is this all going to happen? (the fine print)

How Much Should You Offer?

There is no golden rule for this part. At times you may think you want to offer the lowest price maybe even a laughable amount just to see if they're desperate or want a lower starting point. Other times you feel like making a higher offer on a property you feel strongly about if only to entice the seller to accept right away.

Here are some tips that meet in the middle.

- Work fast. Sometimes this means being the first to put up an offer. Try and set up alerts with your realtor so you can know as soon as a new property is listed. The key is not to hesitate!
- Offer more earnest money. The standard amount is 1% - 2% is the customary amount but if you offer more than that it will show the seller just how serious you are about the property. But, if you go this

way, I wouldn't recommend waiving the inspection and financing contingency.
- Submit a letter. It doesn't have to be fancy, just something simple stating your name, offer, and your intentions with the property. If you want to go that extra mile, consider adding a photo of yourself and a little blurb about yourself to let them know it's a person buying the property and not a corporation. If you're financing, be proactive and include a pre-approval letter from the bank with your offer, so the seller knows that you qualify, and the sale *will* go through if chosen.
- Sellers love to see cash. All cash will make your offer more appealing even if others have offered more because the money is there and the risk of backing out is minimized.
- Remove the financing contingency. This can put you at risk of losing your earnest money deposit if you're financing and the loan falls through so it's a risk, but this risk will most likely get that "yes" you want.
- Waive the inspection contingency to make your offer stand out. It's a calculated risk, but most sellers will already know about what's wrong with their property and don't

like it showing up on inspections that can tank a sale or drop the price. Some houses collect a lot of junk and cleaning them out can be a pain, try offering to clean the house for the seller.
- More earnest money. Consider offering more earnest money up front this will show the seller you are serious about your offer. 1% - 2% is standard but offering another percentage or two would show the seller how dedicated your are. But when offering more earnest money DON'T remove the contingencies or if you have to back out due to some unforeseen issue then you could be out quite a bit of money.
- Escalation clause. Basically this is a clause that is put into the contract that says if someone bids higher than me then automatically raise the price by X number of dollars above theirs, to a certain predetermined value you have decided on. This is a good tactic when you know you are bidding against multiple offers. But never go any higher than you are comfortable with and knowing what the property is valued at.
- Are they looking for a fast close or getting the most dollars? Once you know their

motivation it's easier to tailor your offer to something accepted right away.
- If your offer is turned down, try again, it doesn't mean you can't go back with another offer at a later date. Wait a month or two, and if it's still on the market, the seller might be more motivated to accept your original offer or go lower.

One last thing to consider when making your offer, while speed is generally going to be your friend when it comes to snagging that perfect property, the opposite could also be said. Look for properties that have been on the market for some time. You can tell this by their MLS number (all properties listed on MLS are given a listing number) for example if most of the properties you are looking at the start with 382*** but you notice some properties are 380*** then that could signify it's been on the market a while. You may be able to offer them a much lower price than the listed price.

Remember: Making an offer is a big deal. It can be stressful and cause some sleepless nights. However, to start your real estate empire you have to get off the sidelines and start making offers or your dream of financial freedom will only ever be that.

Chapter 8: Negotiations

Now that you've made your offer *and* it's been accepted, the next step is negotiations. As this is not something you do every day and you may not be very comfortable in this position, but learning to negotiate is an art form and one that you will need to tailor as you travel down the investment path. You don't want to be the person who always pays full price or lays down for a high-baller. You want to be the top dog who always maximizes your cash flow. Let's get to work.

Negotiation Process

The next part of the process is a little harder and something you have no control over. Waiting for the seller to respond.

Picture this, you find a property you really like and want to make an offer on but as you research the comparables in the area you realize that the seller has overpriced the property. Let's say the building is priced at $550,000 but comparables in the area over the last six months have sold for between $475,000 and $500,000 and upon some initial inspection you see that the property does need some work. What now? Well, you could walk away. But you now like to see problems as challenges so instead you write up an offer closer to the low end comparable ($480,000) knowing you will have to do some repairs to get in ready for rental. The seller may ignore the offer or they may counter. For the sake of this example let's say they counter back with an offer of $540,000. Still higher than you would like but now you know the seller is willing to bargain.

Now you have a couple of options. Counter a slightly higher price than your original offer but still lower than they want and put in some data to prove why you are offering low, fixing the roof costs "x", the windows need replacing and the cost "x" so you're deducting that from the offer price. Or you can counter closer to what they are asking *if* they are willing to fix these issues before closing.

Again, for the sake of this example you counter with the first option, only slightly higher ($495,000) with the data to show the repairs that are required. The seller disagrees with your assessment and counters with $525,000 but willing to fix up a couple of minor issues.

We are getting closer.

You accept the minor fixes but still want the roof fixed before closing so counter one more time offering $510,000 if the seller will fix the roof and the other issues before closing.

The seller agrees. You are now the proud owner of a new piece of property.

So the seller will respond one of three ways:

- Accept it - Yay! This is the answer you wanted.
- Reject it - Boo! That's ok, now you can move on to other deals or wait and resubmit down the road.
- Counter it - Usually, the seller will come back an offer that is lower than their asking price but higher than your offer.

Coming back with a counter is a good thing. It signifies that the seller wants to sell to you, so it's best to see the positive side and try to meet in the middle so that both of you end up happy with the outcome. Never get too aggressive or insulting with what the seller counters with.

Think of countering as a way that both parties can walk away from the deal happy and having achieved what they wanted. These negotiations don't just refer to price. It also refers to the closing date, possession date, contingencies, closing costs, repairs, and many other things. Anything and everything can be on the table for discussion, the possibilities are endless.

When to Negotiate

The most intense and heated negotiations can happen immediately after submitting your first offer. You may take turns countering until one of you walks away or you start to meet in the middle and come to an offer that works for you both.

If the inspection reveals any kind of defects, especially one you weren't expecting, this is when you can back out *if* you have an inspection contingency in your offer or you can look at negotiating on the repair costs. Maybe you ask the seller to have the repairs fixed before closing, maybe you ask the seller to lower the price to make up for the repair costs you will have to spend upon closing.

The reality is negotiating can happen at any point along the process. Think about it this way, you negotiate every day in some small way, whether it is with your spouse, your kids or colleagues, negotiating a fair price is no different. It doesn't have to be at the beginning and it doesn't have to be after the inspection, it can be ongoing which builds more trust between you and the seller making them more likely to meet you halfway.

Tips for Successful Negotiations

- Always get the last concession, similar to getting the last word in a disagreement. For everything the seller asks for during the negotiation, you agree. Even if they want you to pay an exorbitant amount more than you offered, say ok but still only pay the closing costs. Always find a way to ask for something of the seller when they counter. Eventually, they will see that anytime they require something, so will you, this makes short work of dissolving any confusion.
- Knowing your role is important when in multiple-offer competitions. You don't want to come in guns blazing with your offer or concessions when the seller has three other offers on the table. You'll end up looking foolish before you even begin. Long story short, know what you're walking into and act accordingly.

- Negotiate with information and have comparables at the ready. When possible hit the seller with data you gathered about similar properties in the neighborhood, especially when you can't seem to find common ground on a price. It's hard to argue with facts and it may bring the seller down back down to earth.
- Use the tactic of gathering information to find out the seller's true motivations for selling. Are they looking for a quick close? Do they need to move and don't want to deal with an out of state property? Is it due to a spousal death and they simply don't need a big house or want to be reminded of the memories anymore? Whatever their reasons, try to appease them while still getting what you want in the process.
- Institute a penalty. When the seller comes back to you with concessions institute a penalty but that I mean taking your time to respond to their counter or if they counter with an amount higher than you want, you say fine but and add in something that you will expect for that higher price, and each time they ask for something, you also ask for something in return. Eventually they will stop asking for things as they will

begin to realize that asking for things means possibly having to give up something else and could hurt their bottom line.
- Ask for their lowest price, then go lower. If you are negotiating with a motivated seller try asking what their absolute lowest price is. Usually, this isn't really their lowest number, but if you were to say "If I could pay you all cash and close in the next couple of weeks how would that sound?" This gives you a better shot at a successful purchase. In just a few short moments you will have been able to talk then down from their "lowest" price and potentially save yourself thousands of dollars.
- Real estate is all about the numbers. A seller wants to get the best dollar for their investment property and you want to get the best deal. If you run the numbers on a property and have offered the best you can to make a profit, divulge this information to the seller. It's hard to argue against the cold hard numbers.

Don't get offended, and always be ready to walk away. When you don't need something as much as the other person, your position becomes stronger, especially when they realize you will walk away if you don't get the right deal. This is easier to say than it is to practice, especially for new investors, but you need to try and remain unattached. If you become desperate for the deal you are lost. Remember this is a game so stay focused, don't get your feelings hurt and always keep it light-hearted.

Chapter 9: Due Diligence

"The real test is not whether you avoid this failure, because you won't. It's whether you let it harden or shame you into inaction, or whether you learn from it; whether you choose to persevere." - Barack Obama

This comes after an offer has been accepted but before you take ownership of the property. This is the time to start verifying title searches, documents on income and expenses, and doing a physical floor by floor or unit by unit, fine-tooth comb inspection. At the end of the day, you wouldn't buy a car off the internet or by just kicking the tires. You would take it for a test drive and have a mechanic check it out. So never spend your hard-earned money or sign on the dotted line without a full inspection. Always check "under the hood" of your real estate investment.

Title Search

Completing a title search should show if there are any liens or outstanding mortgages on the property as you don't want to finish the sale and then come to find out there is a hidden lien. That will cause significant problems for you. You want a "clear title," and so does the bank. The definition of a lien is "a legal claim or a right against a property." They provide security for the bank or the private lender when a legal obligation hasn't been met. It allows a person or organization to take legal action to satisfy debts and obligations. Liens prevent the property from being sold to another buyer without the debt owed being paid to the appropriate parties first.

The reason for the title search is to make sure that there are no liens on the property before purchase. You will want the title company or an attorney, who is dealing with the closing to perform the title closing search as it is different for each State and Province. If you're not sure, you can check with local investors to see how it's done.

Regardless of where you are in the world, your real estate agent will probably have an inside track on who to use and should be able to recommend someone if you don't already have a favorite.

The attorney or title company will get to work on researching the chain of title and get you some title insurance as well. This insurance is similar to house or car insurance in that it will protect you as it covers any issues such as due diligence, not turning up a mortgage already in place. The insurance will cover any financial damage caused by this hidden information.

If you're buying without an agent, then it's up to you to contact the title company so they can start the research. If you're paying cash, you could probably get away with not doing a title search, but that isn't recommended. You never know what could come back to bite you down the road.

Document Inspection

Depending on the type of property you are purchasing and its previous use, there could either be little to no documents for review or quite a bit. The point of the inspection is to verify the information the seller is claiming about the property. Let's get started.

The seller's disclosure statement is a stack of documents they provide with all of the information about the property and any pre-existing issues. The caveat to this is it's only what they know, and there could be serious issues that were overlooked. On top of whatever information they find pertinent, you should ask for at least 24 months of income and expense statements. Also, make a note of the operating budget, look at any unusual expenses or major periods of rent loss, and discuss these findings with the seller or broker before the due diligence period ends.

Obtain the seller's tax returns. This should be an accurate representation of how the property performs because it is unlikely that the seller would inflate numbers only to owe the Internal Revenue Service (IRS) or Canada Revenue Agency (CRA) more taxes. Look for any discrepancies between what was filed and what the seller has provided you.

Service agreements. Look for termination clauses that are greater than 30 days. Most companies only require a written 30-day notice for canceling a contract. Why are these greater? Look at the operating budget and notice what services might be missing or unnecessary. Assess the current management company; should they stay or go? Check any advertising agreements for effectiveness. It is worth your time to look at all the agreements as you will be taking them on and could be locked in. You need to it out before completion of the due diligence period ending.

Current years property tax bill - You can verify this online or by calling the assessor's office or local city hall where the bills are paid.

Current leases - If the property is already rented with existing tenants, then you want to know what agreements are in place as you will be assuming these. Pay close attention to the rental rate, the length of the contract, and any out-of-the-ordinary terms.

Current rent roll - You want to verify the actual income, the actual potential income, and the future potential income. Take a hard look at every unit that is under market rent. These will be your "golden egg" that can increase your cash flow quickly after purchase.

Security deposits - If the property is already rented, then this is the time that you want to verify and examine the security deposits. Approving these should be non-negotiable, especially when purchasing multi-family buildings. You want to know exactly what it covers as the terms are binding once you take over as landlord. Read them carefully and don't assume that anything is or looks boilerplate, scrutinize it, and have your lawyer look over them as well. Verify to make sure you are given the correct amount at closing. If the seller has interest accrued on the deposits, then collect this from them as well.

Current or recent maintenance - This will give you an idea of the work that has been done to maintain the property and any action that still needs attention. Did the seller defer any maintenance to make the expenses appear to be less than they really are?

Utilities - Verify that you have all the utility bills. Call the companies and get the previous 12 months of operating history on each account. Ask about possible increases for the next year. Insert the revised numbers into your budget.

Payroll information - For larger properties, you will want to look at who works there and how much they are being paid. When assuming employees treat them like new hires as you are not familiar with them. Verify vacation time (earned and accrued). Consider doing credit and criminal background checks.

HOA/Strata documents - If HOA or Strata runs the property then you want to know what kinds of conditions they have on the property. Have any special assessments been put through? What work do they on the books coming up in the next year? Do they have any rental restrictions? Some HOA/Strata properties have a no rental policy, and some cap the number of rentals to a percentage. You don't want to buy and then realize you can't rent out your unit because it's not allowed or they have reached their allowable limit.

Physical Inspection

Are you ready to get a little dirty?

Just as you can't judge a book by its cover, you shouldn't judge a building by its outward appearance as they can be deceiving. You need to get to the bones and see what lies beneath. There can be an incredible amount of risks that, if not found in time, could cause substantial amounts of loss down the line.

Walkthrough the property on your own and see what you can find in terms of any red flags that jump out at you, but *do not* inspect it yourself. Hire a professional house/building inspector. Ask your realtor for a recommendation or check out: ashi.org (US) to find someone local who can do the work for you.

Speed is of the essence at this point as you will most likely not have a lot of time left in your due diligence period to complete this, and the inspector will need a few days to get their final report back to you. You will need time to read over the information and think about what to do next.

If the property is unoccupied, make sure the water, power, and any other utilities are turned on. The inspector won't be able to find leaks or broken switches/wiring if the utilities aren't on.

You don't need to be there on inspection day, but I recommend being there to walk around with the inspector and ask questions. The reports can be long and technical. By being there and asking questions, you will know what the inspector means when they write, "illegal and dangerous wiring in the second bedroom." It could be a matter of crossed wires, and you or an electrician could fix that in 30 seconds.

The inspector will look at everything:

- Foundation/crawl space including slab, posts, beams, and joists
- Rot
- Rodents
- Past repairs

- Condition of doors, windows, walls, and flooring
- Cabinets and drawers
- Plumbing
- Electrical
- Outlets
- Heating source
- Attic and/or basement
- Roof
- Chimney/fireplace
- Gutters and downspouts
- Landscaping

Afterward, you will receive a lengthy report on their findings, especially if you're buying an older home. It's their job to find any potential hazards and your duty to decide which issues are essential and what can wait. Inspections can be costly depending on the size of the property but think of them as an investment in peace of mind for knowing all you can about the property.

Other Inspections You May Want to Consider

There are not as commonly done and will depend on the type of property you are buying, but in the long run, they could save you a lot of money.

- Plumbing - Inspectors check to look for leaks and can test if the water runs and drains well, but they can't see inside them. Consider hiring a plumber or plumbing inspector as they can stick a camera down the drains and look for cracks in the pipes.
- Asbestos - This is a naturally occurring fibrous material that can be deadly. However, it's only dangerous if it's disturbed, i.e., if you're planning on any renovations. While it is present in hundreds of different products, it is most commonly found in pipe insulation. Attic insulation known as Vermiculite and exterior siding. Most commonly used before the 1990's, it has since been outlawed in many places.
- Environmental Assessments - If looking to purchase a commercial property, it's worth considering having a Phase I Environmental Assessment completed. These reports look for PCBs, Asbestos, underground storage tanks, lead-based paint, etc. Most of those are not issues unless they will be disturbed during renovations or have already been disturbed in some fashion due to age. At that point, a Phase II Environmental

Assessment will need to be completed. If this is your first property, I would probably walk away at this point. Cleanups can be expensive, and once remediation starts you don't know what else you might find that could cost big bucks.
- Lead-Based Paint - Very unlikely, but before colonial times lead-based paint was used in many interior and exterior walls because of its resistance to moisture and low cost. It was eventually found to be harmful to the human nervous system and outlawed in 1978. If you are buying an older home and considering any renovations, I would recommend having some of the surfaces tested. You can hire a company to do this for you, or test kits are available in most home improvement stores.
- Pests - Termites, carpenter ants, and other wood-eating bugs can create havoc and thousands of dollars worth of structural damage long before anyone even knows they are there. If your inspection turns up evidence of these pests, I would recommend hiring a pest control company to come in and dig a little deeper into the potential problem. Pun intended.

After the Inspection

At this point, you should have all the information you need to make an educated decision about purchasing your property. I cannot stress enough that you need to verify, verify, verify. You don't want to be in a position after closing on a "great" property only to find out that you are the proud owner of a money pit. With such a small due diligence window, it's up to you to handle the investigative work with some help from your realtor and the long list of able-bodied professionals available online.

Chapter 10: Closing the Sale

"Success is not the key to happiness. Happiness is the key to success. If you love what you are doing, you will be successful." - Albert Schweitzer

You are now one step closer to owning your rental property, but there are some crucial next steps before getting the keys.

The key to the rest of the process is preparation. The way you set up your rental business before you close on your properties will determine the success of your business and as a landlord. This chapter will be spent on preparation. The things you should do (or consider doing) before closing on your property. This stuff is far from glamorous, but it could save you financial strife. What to consider before closing the sale:

Insurance

Fires, floods, and water leaks can happen, and in most cases, they *do* happen eventually. So you want to make sure you are prepared with an adequate amount of insurance coverage before closing. As you did when searching for your house insurance, you need to get quotes, compare, pick one, and request that a "binder" be sent to the attorney or title/escrow company handling the closing. Just be sure to check your math and plan for it in your budgeting.

Insurance for Landlords

This is an expense most investors wish they could skip, but the thought of watching all of your hard work and money go up in flames because you didn't buy insurance should scare you straight. There is a range of different policies depending on where you are in the US, so check with your insurance broker for the best ones.

For homes that are older and need some fixing up, the choice may be made for you in terms of being limited to only an Actual Cash Value (ACV) policy. This means the insurance company only has to give you enough insurance money to cover what you paid minus the value of the land that it sits on.

This policy may not ever pay out enough to cover major damages if you need to rebuild. The worst-case scenario would be only having enough coverage to pay off the loan and be left with a vacant lot. Still, any policy is better than none and might be worth a small loss, especially if you are willing to pay a slightly higher deductible or do some of the repair work yourself to rebuild. It's important to note that some ACV does not cover water damage from frozen or damaged pipes.

A replacement cost policy is preferred if you can get it. The coverage is better and will pay for the full cost of covered losses (minus your deductible), sometimes even covering a full rebuild of the house. But to qualify for this coverage, the house *must* be in good condition. That means a nearly new roof and siding, a pristine yard, and no cracked paint.

When looking at coverage, make sure it includes a large enough payout to rebuild the house or structure based on what contractors in your area charge. The number may not even be close to what you paid, it can be significantly more or less, but you need to be covered. What you paid is irrelevant; what it costs to rebuild is.

Make sure you insure for full replacement value. There are cheaper options, but then you could be on the hook for the balance of the replacement. For example: If the value of your property is

$200,000, but you only insure it for $100,000, that's only 50% of the value. If something goes wrong, let's say a toilet overflows and causes $4,000 worth of damages, then the insurance company would only payout 50% of the cost, $2,000 minus your deductible.

Next, make sure your insurance covers any outbuildings if there are any on the property such as a shed or garage, barn, pool, or cottage. This will be anything that is not attached to the primary residence.

Also, look for "loss of rents" coverage. This covers the rent you would have received from tenants, if for example, there's a fire, and they have to live elsewhere while the building is being repaired.

Finally, make sure you have liability insurance. This is for such things as someone suing you if they get hurt on your property. Common limits are $300,000, $500,000, and $1,000,000, but you can get higher limits, and they don't cost much more.

Renters will need personal/tenants insurance to cover their assets against fire and theft or in case they are found to be liable or negligent if they hurt themselves. It's nice for your insurance company to have something to bill against. Consider making that a requirement for all new tenants.

Setting Up Your Bank Accounts

Always keep your rental property expenses separate from your expenses. Make sure to have a savings and checking account for your rental property as the savings account is where you would deposit any damage deposit checks. The reason for the savings account is some States and Province require the landlord to pay out interest on the damage deposit to the tenant at the time of departure. You need to be able to easily calculate that amount owed back to the tenant minus any clean up you may need to do on the unit once the tenant is gone. Setting up a separate account for the deposit checks makes this easier. Make sure to set them up well in advance of closing the deal as it can take time to get checks and debit cards in the mail. Never use a personal check to pay for a business expense. Mixing them up will be an accounting nightmare and make it much more complicated than it needs to be.

Also, make sure to have a system in place that works for paying with checks versus a debit card and to track spending. The simplest way is to have the tenant mail you the check. Still, in this day and age of technology, there are apps or software programs geared towards landlords and property management companies to be able to assist with this, which I will cover under the additional resources section.

Forms

If you plan on managing everything yourself for a while, there are forms you will need for operations. If you like to keep carbon copies I suggest purchasing a filing cabinet to help with organization and to have at least six copies of each form in a designated file, so you aren't scrambling to find a blank template every time someone moves in.

If you are like everyone else in the modern age and prefer technology, you can always use "The Cloud" to store your documents. In the simplest terms, "The Cloud" means storing and accessing data over the internet without accessing a computer hard-drive. The Cloud is just a metaphor for the web. Google Drive is fantastic for this because you can create folders and upload forms within Google Drive, which has features that resemble Word and Excel but are virtual. What that means is you have access from anywhere, including being able to retrieve documents and sign them on your tablet or smartphone.

Whether you prefer handwriting, digital copies or both, you need the following forms on hand that is required by your state, city or county:

- Application
- Rental minimum qualifications form
- Month-to-month lease
- Annual lease
- Deposit to hold agreement
- Property rules and regulations
- Adverse action notice
- Notice for landlord or maintenance to enter a unit
- 20 or 30 days notice to end the tenancy (whichever is required by your state)
- Move-in/move-out packet
- Cleaning expectations
- New tenant checklist
- Move-in/move-out condition report
- Pet addendum
- Tenant reference questionnaire
- Disposition of deposit
- Mold and mildew disclosure form

Preparing Bookkeeping

You can choose an accounting software package such as QuickBooks, Sage or Freshbooks or use an online property management tool such as AppFolio.com or Verticalrent.com

Another option would be to use Excel or Google Sheets, which integrate with Google Drive to track all your income and expenses. However, if you're like me and not comfortable with doing your accounting or numbers just aren't your thing, then consider hiring an accountant to do it for you.

To LLC or Not to LLC

That is the question.

Well, the simple answer is "talk to an attorney," but there are some benefits and downfalls of having a limited liability company, and you should decide what is right for you. I'm sure you've heard stories of landlords getting sued by a tenant or tenants and losing their shirts. That's not to say that having an LLC prevents this from happening, but an LLC helps manage the fallout of such an event occurring. These are hybrid legal structures that provide the limited liability features of a corporation and the tax efficiencies of a partnership.

LLC Benefits

- Limited liability - If you get sued, your liability could be contained to the assets under the LLC, not everything you own. But make sure every 'T' is crossed and every 'i' is dotted, because there are ways a judge can get through the LLC to get at your personal property if they found you negligent or in the wrong.
- Tax efficiency - No corporate tax, which means tax time is easier and less expensive as the income and expenses just "pass-through" magically and are reported by each member on their income statement.
- Operational flexibility - Flexible in terms of running it. It can be set up easily and inexpensively and only requires a few documents as opposed to the thousands you might need to set up a corporation.

Problems with an LLC

Most residential lenders (lenders who loan on small unit properties) won't lend to an LLC, which means turning to commercial lenders who have higher fees, higher rates, and shorter lending terms.

You could get the loan in your name and then transfer the loan to your LLC afterward, but once the bank finds out, they could call your loan "due" because of the "due on sale" clause. Now you didn't really sell the property, but the banks don't see it that way, and with interest rates rising, they are getting stickier about that clause compared with past years and lower interest rates when they would turn a blind eye to it. If this is a route you would like to go, consider talking with the bank about getting permission and getting it in writing. That should protect you from the "due on sale" clause.

What are you protecting? Most likely, this is your first or second property, but in any event, you probably haven't built up much equity yet. The reality is for so little equity, it's a lot of paperwork and hassle. While LLCs are easier than corporations, they can get complicated. Setting it up takes capital, maintaining it takes money, and so does filing taxes, especially with multiple members as an individual return needs to be done by each member. An LLC comes in handy *when* you have wealth to protect, and by then, you should have a team in place to set it up for you.

Chapter 11: You Own, So What's Next?

"If you can dream it, you can do it." - Walt Disney

Congratulations! You are now the proud owner of a rental property. Now that you have navigated the world of real estate to purchase some property, you must not slow down. If anything, you must ramp up the work or all the time, money, and every put in could be jeopardized by not managing the property correctly. The first question you must ask yourself is, are you going to manage the property, or are you going to hire a company to do so for you?

Self Management vs. Property Management Company

As I've stated throughout this book, there is no one right answer to whether you should do this yourself or hire someone. Everyone has different skills, personalities, and availability. If you're going to attempt this alone, can you manage all the ins and outs while working a full-time job? If you opted for a partnership based on your skills, can you successfully split tasks?

Role of a Property Manager

This is a hard role to define as most will perform a variety of tasks depending on what you require of them and what you determine from the beginning. Here are the most common things that a property manager is responsible for:

- Advertising vacant units
- Screening applicants
- Approving tenants
- Signing leases
- Handling all phone calls from tenants
- Scheduling maintenance
- Issuing late notices
- Filing eviction notices
- Keeping records of income and expenses

Pros

- Clears up your day to do the things you weren't able to do with a 9-5 schedule.

- Always have reliable contractors at the ready, and you may get a bulk discount on work.
- Already has an infrastructure in place to handle your rental and a system to find new tenants.
- It gives you time to focus on looking for other property acquisition deals.

Cons

- Price. The management fees can eat into your cash flow by up to 10%, depending on where you live. Some may even charge a fee of up to 50% for new tenant move-ins. If going this route, remember to factor the cost into your budget and run the numbers carefully. Where you once thought you would be getting an ROI of 12% that could dip below 6% when factoring in all the company fees. Is the free time they offer by doing the work for you worth it to you in the long run?
- Designated problem solver. Almost every day, something new will come up that needs attention or fixing, especially if you own multiple properties. How are you at problem-solving?

- Managing staff. Even if you do the bulk of the work yourself, you can't be everywhere at once, so having people on staff to help is a good idea — either a leasing agent, a maintenance person, or the property management company itself.

No One Will Care Like You

This is a tick in the column for managing the property yourself. No one will care about the property the way that you will. You will only have one or two properties to manage, whereas a property management company could have hundreds or thousands to manage. Your property will not be special to them, and neither will your tenants.

If you have a company, your job will not be passive, and you will still need to look out for your tenants. Stay on top of the manager to make sure that they aren't overcharging your tenants and that they are keeping up with any issues.

If you decide to go the route of hiring a property manager, make sure to vet them just as you would your tenants. Treat it like a job interview and ask the tough questions. Referrals are very important in this scenario.

Self Management

Treat it like a business. If you only give it partial attention as you would a hobby, then you won't last long in the real estate rental business. For long term success, you need to set it up as you would any other business with official hours, rules, and standards, etc.

Owning a business means having rules and enforcing them. No late payments on rental fees. Set boundaries and make others abide by them as well. This means not getting involved in anyone's personal lives unless it is a threat to others.

Get the Property Ready to Rent

Now whether you decide to hire a property manager or manage it yourself, always rehab the property first before renting it out. The reality is that once people are living there, it will be almost impossible to do any large scale renovations. Not to mention, you are likely to get tenants that don't care about the state of where they live, which means they won't keep it up as well.

Paint, clean, change out the kitchen hardware, make sure all the appliances work and perform any other task that you felt needed doing during your due diligence phase. Once complete, make sure to take pictures of the interior and exterior for reference after the tenant moves out, and they are asking for their deposit back.

You have now successfully gotten your property ready for the market.

Congratulations!

Chapter 12: Additional Resources

I thought it might be helpful to have a section dedicated to extra resources for you to use as a reference. This way you won't have to search through all of the information I have provided in this book when looking for something specific. It's not exhaustive as there is so much information out there but it should help you narrow down some of the information you will need to make some informed decisions.

Accounting

Quickbooks.intuit.com - A rental property and personal financial management tool. It enables users to track tenant information, manage income and track expenses. It offers items such as credit checks, tax and expense management and allows users to categorize their personal and rental property expenses easily.

Sage.com (Canada) - Accounting integration with Office365. Manages invoicing, cash flow, payments, and taxes. Is also available across all devices.

Freshbooks - It can automate tasks such as invoicing, organizing your expenses, and tracking your time. As FreshBooks lives in the Cloud you can easily and securely access it from any computer, smartphone or tablet. Simple, intuitive, and easy to use.

Canada Revenue Agency (CRA) - https://www.canada.ca/en/revenue-agency.html - all things tax related for personal and business forms and questions for Canadians.

Internal Revenue Service (IRS) - https://www.irs.gov/ - all things tax related for personal and business forms and questions for Americans.

Property Management

ww.softwareadvice.com/property - During my research I came across this website that offers reviews on approx 126 different types of property management and financial websites for landlords, property managers, brokers, etc. It also shows you the cost of the software and if it's for small businesses or large business. I listed a couple below that I found to be quite good.

appfolio.com - Good for small, medium or large businesses, it's an all in one mobile app that allows you to keep track of applications, requests, accounting, vacancies, and renters insurance, just to name a few.

buildingstack.com (Canada) - It enables users to organize current vacancies and lease agreements, receive online rental payments, track the progress of units under repair. It also posts vacancies automatically to sites like Kijiji.

tenantcloud.com - Offers user's property management, tenant management, and accounting management. Tracks lease expirations, new transactions, total occupancy, and outstanding rent payments. It also allows for direct messaging to tenants to address any issues or ask questions.

Building Inspectors

I mentioned that when looking for an inspector talk to your real estate agent as they may have someone they work with regularly and trust. You can use these companies as a back-up to their advice.

ashi.org (US) American Society of Home Inspectors has an exhaustive list of inspectors and checklists. The website also has plenty of information and resources on what the inspectors look for and why, check out the Resources tab for information on Electrical, Interiors, Insulation, etc.

cahpi.ca (Canada) Canadian Association of Home and Property Inspectors also has an exhaustive list of inspectors and resources. Where to find a home inspector, new construction inspectors, and much much more.

Miscellaneous

www.biggerpockets.com/real-estate-investment-calculator - This site is designed to help you quickly analyze the potential on any property for profitability. It has 7 different calculators to assist with different property options. For example a mortgage calculator, a fix and flip calculator, as well as a rental property calculator.

ratehub.ca (Canada) - A website designed to help you compare rates on anything from credit cards to investing and mortgages.

moneycrashers.com - Blog on anything from family and home, investing and loans.

investopedia.com - another website/blog with lots of great information on investing, financing, pros and cons of real estate, etc.

Google Voice (US) - A telephone service that provides call forwarding and voicemail services. It provides a US number but can be accessed or forwarded to international numbers in Canada, and a handful of European countries. This way people looking to rent call this number but it's forwarded to your cell and then your cell number isn't out there for just anyone to call.

crimereports.com - (Canada and the US) - use this to look up certain areas and what the crime rate may be, the report will only be as accurate as the particular agency (police force) keeps it, but it will give you an idea.

city-data.com (US) - some of the information here is more up to date as of March 2019, other data is from 2017, with similar data such as population size and median earnings.

city-data.com/canada - the information is only up to 2011 but gives an idea of the population, the change in population size, population density, median earnings, and various other measures.

greatschools.org (US only) - this website helps parents find the right school for their family. So something to consider looking into when checking out an area for homes and types of tenants.

dol.gov/general/topic/statistics/unemployment (US Department of Labor) - this site is good for checking out jobs, unemployment rates, and employment projections in various towns, cities, and states.

usa.com/rank - this site looks at best / worst states, fastest / slowest growing states, and richest / poorest counties and states, etc.

bac-lac.gc.bc (Canada census reports) - use this site to check out things like population growth based on the latest census report.

census.gov/construction/nrc (US census) - use this site to check out things like population growth based on the latest census report.

Conclusion

You are now on your way to financial freedom and building your real estate empire. I hope you now have a greater understanding of what it means to be a successful landlord.

But, before I leave you to go and start acquiring all your properties, a few last pieces of advice, as much as this book has talked about the "would be nice" apartment buildings, you should also consider the "wouldn't touch with a ten-foot pole" houses. There is no such thing as a perfect property, but there is sure to be one out there for you *if* you know what you want.

If you are on the hunt for your first property, then I sincerely hope this book has given you the inspiration you need to go out and start pounding the pavement to find that great house or duplex that will start you on your journey to financial freedom.

If you are a seasoned property owner, I hope you gained a little bit of knowledge you didn't have before, and this book inspires you to keep climbing.

Some Last Things to Consider

Property taxes may explode. Always try and have a contingency for your property taxes as they can fluctuate from year to year. Remember that the homeowner's grant will not apply anymore as it's not your primary residence, rentals and supplemental properties are not entitled to any grants, which will mean a significant increase from what you may be used to paying. Consider rent based on possible increases. If possible, add a few percentages to the current rent to make up for the increase each year.

Be prepared for damage. It can happen within a short amount of time, so make sure to check on your property regularly. Don't be a pain to your tenants, but it lets them know your property is taken care of.

In the last few years within some provinces in Canada, there has been an influx of drug labs found within homes, so insurance companies are getting stricter with what they cover. In some provinces, I have heard that you must check on your property every three months to make sure that your insurance remains valid but was unable to find any research that confirms this, so unsure if this is an urban legend or truth. What I did find out was that any damages incurred by a potential drug lab are NOT covered.

Keep an eye out for potential extra bedrooms. Look for spaces that could be converted into an additional bedroom. Keywords in a listing that say "large bedroom," "attic" or "bonus room" can be a treasure trove for innovative renovations. The large bedroom could be split into two; the attic or bonus room could be converted into a spare room. Suddenly your two-bedroom is now a three-bedroom, and you have increased the value of your property.

Repairs are expensive and can be unexpected. Set up an emergency fund to cover these. Understand that in the beginning, while you are building up your equity and resources, you may be out of pocket for some of these repairs, and they could come at the worst time possible, but make sure to set money aside from rent for these. Don't let the unknown control you, take control of the situation, and prepare for the unexpected.

Good tenants will be worth their weight in gold. Good or even great tenants will take liberties to care for your property and maybe also improve it. This means less time on your part and fewer repairs. Doing your due diligence to find these tenants will pay you back in the long run.

It's challenging buying property, but being a landlord will be an even bigger challenge. Tenants will test you. The property will test you. Screen your tenants thoroughly and carefully. Keep an eye on the property frequently. Be respectful of the families you rent to, but don't be afraid to lay down the law. Rent is due on time, or fees will apply, for example. You're a landlord, and you need to let the tenants know that rules matter.

Final Thoughts

If this is your first investment property, I'm going to suggest that a single-family home or condo might be your best bet.

Condos are considered lower maintenance as the HOA or Strata council takes care of all the common areas, which leaves you to only care for the interior of your unit. However, the downside to condos is the market value may not allow for very high rents, and they appreciate slower than a single-family home.

To this, I can attest, I had a condo in a very "hot" market, yet even after some small renovations, I wasn't able to even get close to market value for the rent when I moved, and then when it came time to sell I had to sell for less than the assessed value. As it had been my primary residence, first, there was an emotional attachment, and not being able to get the value I wanted was a hard pill to swallow.

I learned something valuable here. You can never guess what the market will bear when it comes time to sell, while you may feel it's worth a certain dollar value to you, the market is the final say on what it's actually worth. Sure, you can hold out for the price you want, or you let it go and move on to the next property. Many more level headed businesspersons can remove themselves from attachment and consider the profit and loss of selling now or holding on and selling later. Not me, at first.

While I struggled with the idea of having to sell as it had been my first home purchase, I soon realized I didn't have the luxury of waiting for the market to catch up to condos. I was operating at a loss each month due to charging far too little for rent and not being able to catch up with increases as I was only able to add 3% a year. So I eventually cut my losses and sold.

What I hope to impart with my story is this:

I didn't know what it meant to be a landlord and own property, so I didn't take it seriously and as such, had to cut my losses. The goal for more real estate investors is to increase their income as passively as possible. So always make sure your units are rented out at market value, not below. Do your research before setting a price. I didn't do my research. I believed everything the property manager told me about the market, putting on added pressure I didn't need. I was desperate to fill my unit as moving to a new city left me with no time to adequately market and show my space to find the right tenant.

The flip side of this is to be aware of not charging too much. You want to make money but not at the expense of your tenants or your integrity. Charging too much could run the risk of vacancies, which isn't suitable for cash flow. While vacancies are a normal part of owning rentals, you don't want it to be because you are charging too much.

However, should you find yourself in the position of having to fill units, maybe consider a slight decrease in rent to fill a space quickly.

I also didn't have a plan for my unit and being a landlord, which is most likely why it wasn't a successful endeavor for me. Throughout this book, we've talked about having a plan and tying that back to your 'why.' Review your plan, your goals, and your why regularly - daily, monthly, quarterly - whatever makes sense for you to be able to stay on track with your vision. Remember to be flexible. Life happens. Things will happen that may throw you off track, but keep working your plan and don't give up.

At the beginning of the book, I talked about action, and that without work, you're just a dreamer. Without effort, you will stay where you are in more ways than one. I've given you tips and a road map on how to purchase properties to launch your real estate investing journey.

Don't sit on the bench and watch others play the game. Get out there and have some fun.

Happy hunting and keep building that real estate empire.

Finally, if you found this book useful in any way, a review on Amazon is always appreciated!

Citations

Kennon, Joshua (2019). Real Estate Investing. Retrieved from https://www.thebalance.com/real-estate-investing-101-357985

Keller, Gary with Jenks, Dave & Papasan, Jay (2005). The Millionaire Real Estate Investor (PDF)

Gallinelli, Frank (2005). Insider Secrets to Financing Your Real Estate Investments (PDF)

McElroy, Ken (2012). The ABC's of Real Estate Investing (PDF)

Tanzer, Mitt (2002). How to Invest in Real Estate with No Money Down (PDF)

Turner, Brandon (2015) The Book on Rental Property Investing (PDF)

Kiyosaki, Robert (2009) The Real Book of Real Estate

Chen, James (2018) Capitilization Rate Definition. Retrieved from https://www.investopedia.com/terms/c/capitalizationrate.asp

Davis, Marc and Grant, Mitchell (2019) Finding Your Return on Real Estate. Retrieved from https://www.investopedia.com/articles/basics/11/calculate-roi-real-estate-investments.asp

Hogan, Chris (n.d.). How to Invest in Real Estate. Retrieved from https://www.daveramsey.com/blog/how-to-invest-in-real-estate

Tips on Rental Real Estate Income, Deductions, and Recordkeeping (n.d.). Retrieved from https://www.irs.gov/businesses/small-businesses-self-employed/tips-on-rental-real-estate-income-deductions-and-recordkeeping

Various pages on the CRA website (2019). Retrieved from https://www.canada.ca/en/revenue-agency/services/tax/businesses/topics/rental-income/capital-cost-allowance-rental-property.html

Johnson, Holly (2017). What I Wish I Knew Before Buying. Retrieved from https://www.thesimpledollar.com/what-i-wish-we-knew-before-buying-rental-property/

Ivy, Michelle (2019). 31 Tips for Buying Your First Property From the Pros. Retrieved from https://fitsmallbusiness.com/buying-your-first-rental-property-tips/

Karrels, Allison (n.d.). Investment Property 101 - Part Two: The Math Behind Investing Retrieved from https://www.listenmoneymatters.com/investment-property-math/

Karrels, Allison (n.d.). Investment Property 101 - Part Three: The Power of Leverage. Retrieved from https://www.listenmoneymatters.com/investment-property-leverage/

https://www.inc.com/jayson-demers/51-quotes-to-inspire-success-in-your-life-and-business.html

Household sizes (2018). Retrieved from https://population.un.org/Household/index.html#/countries/840

Return on Investment information (2019). Retrieved from https://www.merriam-webster.com/dictionary/ROI

www.ingramcontent.com/pod-product-compliance
Lightning Source LLC
Chambersburg PA
CBHW070640220526
45466CB00001B/239